GIANTS
of the
Missionary Trail

The Life Stories of Eight

Men Who Gave Their All

For the Cause of Christ

By EUGENE MYERS HARRISON
B.D., Ph.D.

Foreword by BUD R. CALVERT
D. Min.

Reprinted by:
FAIRFAX BAPTIST TEMPLE
6401 Missionary Lane
Fairfax Station, Virginia

Giants of the Missionary Trail

Copyright © 2010 Fairfax Baptist Temple
6401 Missionary Lane
Fairfax Station, VA 22039
(703) 323-8100

Previous ISBN: 888-021-X
Printed in 1980, 1982, 1990, 1993, 2008

ISBN: 978-0-9829105-7-3
November 2010

Faithful Life Publishers
3335 Galaxy Way
North Fort Myers, FL 33903

www.FaithfulLifePublishers.com

info@FLPublishers.com

Scripture quotations from the King James Version unless otherwise noted.

All rights reserved. No part of this publication may be reproduced, stored in a retrieval system, or transmitted in any form or by any means—electronic, mechanical. photocopy, recording, or any other—except for brief quotations in printed reviews, without the prior permission of Fairfax Baptist Temple or Faithful Life Publishers.

Printed in the United States of America
19 18 17 16 15 14 13 12 11 10   8 9 10 11 12

FOREWORD

When I first read *Giants of the Missionary Trail* I realized I had in my hands a book that God could use to change lives. Since it was out of print Fairfax Baptist Temple received permission to reprint it for the first International Conference on World Evangelism held in Washington, D.C. in 1993. Now we have reprinted it again with the prayer that the Lord will continue to use it as a tool to speak to the hearts of His people.

Giants of the Missionary Trail is an exciting book—one that is difficult to put down once begun. More than that, however, it is intriguing and inspiring as we read of men and women who sacrificed their all for the cause of world evangelism. These giants of the faith will take you with them on their exciting journeys across the ocean to the regions beyond. You will weep with them when they suffer extreme hardship and rejection and rejoice with them when, after years of toil, their first convert is won to Christ or their first church is planted. What could better motivate us to give our lives completely to our Lord than the example of these men and women?

Jeremiah said, "Mine eye affecteth mine heart" (Lamentations 3:51). When God showed him what was to become of Judah he was moved to tears. Jesus said to "Lift up your eyes and look on the fields; for they are white already to harvest" (John 4:35). The challenge presented in these verses is that of a world in dire need of the Gospel of Jesus Christ. We are living in exciting days of opportunity. May what we see in this book move our hearts to action to serve the living God. It is my prayer that some of you will be called to go to a foreign mission field as church planters and missionary wives and that all of us will be encouraged to pray more for our Missionary Evangelists and give more by grace in faith toward their support.

It is the prayer of all of us at Fairfax Baptist Temple that reading the stories of these missionary pioneers and their dedication to the service God will cause you to be more "conformed to the image of His Son," (Romans 8:29) "who gave Himself a ransom for all" (1 Timothy 2:6).

Dr. Bud Calvert
Pastor Emeritus,
Fairfax Baptist Temple
Fairfax, Virginia

OF DRAGONS AND GIANTS

History and literature have much to say—of the depredations of dragons, the tyranny of giants and the heroism of brave men who, defying danger and death, conquered these monsters; of Siegfried who, when the dragon reared to spring upon him, "drove the immortal sword straight into its heart" and went singing on his way to deliver Brunhilde; of St. George who fought valiantly till, on the third day of combat, "the monster fell like a huge rock shattered by a storm;" of Ulysses and his feat of blinding the one-eyed giant, Polyphemus, the monster who gorged himself upon human victims. But the real heroes of history are the spiritual giants who, not in the fanciful pages of mythology or legend, but in actual life, defied death and demons, overcame powerful adversaries, "stopped the mouths of lions, quenched the violence of fire, escaped the edge of the sword, out of weakness were made strong, waxed valiant in fight" and died as conquerors.

The Scriptures, telling of Samson's conquest of a fierce lion, are careful to emphasize the fact that "…he had nothing in his hand." It was then, and only then, that "…the Spirit of the Lord came mightily upon him, and he rent him as he would have rent a kid" (Judges 14:6).

Samson's condition: "…he had nothing in his hand."

Samson's enduement: "…the Spirit of the Lord came mightily upon him."

Samson's triumph: he rent the lion as he would have rent a kid.

Wherein lies the difference between ordinary Christians and extraordinary Christians, between spiritual pygmies and spiritual giants? Simply stated, it is the difference between pre-Pentecost and post-Pentecost. Even after Easter morning, but before Pentecost, the disciples were floundering in a morass of spiritual impotence and cowardice. Between Easter and Pentecost there is not one recorded instance of the disciples making any attempt to preach the Gospel and point lost souls to the Lamb of God. Instead, it is repeatedly stated that they were behind closed doors! They were hiding, not witnessing! But when they paid the cost of Pentecost through the ten days of prayer and contrition in the upper room, and when the mighty fullness of the Holy Spirit came upon them and into them, their cowardice vanished; they threw open the doors and they entered upon a campaign of missionary conquest which is still the glory of the Christian church.

This book tells how God wrote history through the lives of eight men who, like the early disciples, were Giants of the Missionary Trail because they were possessed, filled, controlled and energized by the Holy Spirit of God. This great truth is evidenced in the marvelous ministry of Jonathan Goforth, "The Holy Spirit's Man in China," and all the others portrayed in these pages.

As in several earlier volumes of missionary biographies, I have endeavored to give a faithful account of the conversion, spiritual development, conflicts, trials and triumphs of each missionary, to discover the hidings of power, and to weave all the pertinent data into a pattern of unity and beauty around each character's great life text. It is believed that the questions, topics for study and additional reading suggestions found at the end of each chapter will prove valuable to the individuals making use of them and especially to mission classes and other groups who choose to use this text as a course of study.

Eugene M. Harrison
Wheaton, Illinois

PRELIMINARY COMMENTS AND INSTRUCTIONS FOR THOSE USING THIS VOLUME AS A TEXTBOOK

1. Read straight through the chapter under consideration for a unified view of the missionary. Then read the chapter analytically, keeping in mind the questions and topics for study.

2. In writing these biographies, the author has endeavored to combine three important elements: history, practicality, and inspiration.

3. Only a few questions are asked concerning specific facts; however, a thorough knowledge of factual material is necessary in developing an adequate understanding and appreciation of any character.

4. The author has lifted out of these biographies a number of questions and problems significant to missionary work today in order to stimulate thought and class discussion, as well as research.

5. The supplemental reading assignments should be of value to those who have access to the books cited.

If the books cited are not accessible, you will find much helpful material on religious beliefs and practices in these two books: Ione Lowman's *Non-Christian Religions* and G. H. Smith's *The Missionary and Primitive Man*, both published by Van Kampen Press, Wheaton, Illinois. Smith's book contains much authentic and valuable information concerning primitive, religious ideas, and practices. At last report, it was out of print but may be available in some libraries.

TABLE OF CONTENTS

HENRY NOTT

HERALD OF THE LOVE OF GOD IN TAHITI
(1774 – 1844)

IN THE SHADE of overarching palm trees, on an island in Polynesia, a white man and a native talked. The former was a missionary, the latter a heathen ruler. The white man and his fellow missionaries had been repeatedly threatened with death. Three of them, in fact, had been killed. Four others were assaulted, robbed, stripped and dragged into a stream to be drowned. Managing to escape, they fled across the sea to a remote island accompanied by all the missionaries except one. This lonely but resolute soul was Henry Nott. He had mastered the difficult Tahitian tongue and with toils and tears, had proclaimed his message for more than ten years, but had yet to convert a single native.

Turning to the native king, Henry Nott said: "For the sake of your immortal soul and of your influence upon your subjects, I urge you, for the thousandth time, to turn to Christ. Do not longer reject His glorious salvation. Every human soul is of infinite value to Him."

"Doubtless you are right," replied the swarthy native, "but for one who has sinned so disgracefully and wallowed in the depths of heathen depravities, there is no hope."

"There is hope," rejoined the missionary. And to prove his point he quoted these seraphic syllables: "For God so loved the world that he gave his only begotten Son, that whosoever believeth in him should not perish but have everlasting life" (John 3:16).

Martin Luther called John 3:16 "the little gospel." During his last illness someone recommended to him a certain remedy for his severe headache. He declined with these words: "The best prescription for head and heart is to be found in John 3:16" And in his dying moments, repeated the text three times.

Said Henry Nott, "The only sure and efficacious remedy for the ignorance, the depravities, the sorrows and sins of mankind is to be found in the Gospel of John 3:16."

In appreciation of the sublimities of John 3:16, Martin Luther and Henry Nott were of much the same mind.

I. JOHN 3:16 IS THE ONLY SURE AND EFFICACIOUS REMEDY FOR THE IGNORANCE OF MANKIND.

To establish a mission in Tahiti had, as early as 1787, been the dream of William Carey, the consecrated cobbler who, in 1792, inspired the Baptists to organize the first Foreign Mission Society of modern times. Carey was led instead to India. To Henry Nott, the consecrated brick layer, goes much of the human credit for establishing a mission in Tahiti and throughout the Society Islands. He was born in Bromsgrove in 1774, and was a member of the first company of missionaries sent out by the newly organized London Missionary Society. They sailed on the *Duff* in September, 1796, and reached Tahiti March 5, 1797.

There was much evidence that suggested the Tahitian people were engrossed in strange and dark practices stemming from ignorance and superstition. It was amusing to see the young King Otu and his queen riding on men's shoulders. They were always carried about in this fashion, lest their feet should touch the ground or some other object, because whatever they touched became their own. The official report of the "First Missionary Voyage to the Southern Pacific" published in London, 1799, conveys much astonishing information including the following:

> *The mode of carrying the king and queen is with their legs hanging down before, seated on the shoulders and leaning on the head of their carriers, and very frequently amusing themselves with picking out the vermin which there abound. It is the singular privilege of the queen that, of all women, she alone may eat the vermin, which privilege she never fails to make use of.*

Several years prior to the arrival of the missionaries, two abandoned white men, dissolute sailors, had taken up their abode on the island. Their names were Peter and Andrew. Using these men as interpreters, the missionaries explained to the king why they had come on such a long, perilous journey and inquired whether they would receive his protection in settling among the people. When the objects of the mission had been set forth, the king seemed greatly pleased. He forthwith gave the missionaries the largest house in Tahiti and ceded to them the district known as Matavai. As subsequent events made abundantly clear, the king welcomed the missionaries. He thought their presence would bring him prestige along with a supply of western tools. Not once did he consider their spiritual aims. The king and his people were very generous in furnishing breadfruit, coconuts, hogs and other food for the missionaries, though they always expected generous compensation in the form of axes, and the like.

The most powerful man in Tahiti was a man of powerful physique and of aggressive, dominating personality. By dint of his ferocious courage, he had succeeded in bringing all of Tahiti under one ruler and had extended his sway over a number of other islands.

Pomare was very friendly with the missionaries and often came to see them. He always brought a voracious appetite and regularly stayed to eat. His favorite missionary friend, Henry Nott, watched him devour hearty quantities of fruit and vegetables, along with two chickens and two pounds of pork during a single meal. One of his attendants always fed him; his dignity would not permit him to feed himself. The missionaries were amused "to see so stout a man, perhaps the largest in the whole island, fed like a cuckoo."

One day, Pomare and his wife, Iddeah, came for a visit, perched as usual on men's shoulders. Several of Pomare's attendants carried a large chest. When asked why he brought it, he replied with a smile, "To hold the presents you will be pleased to give me." He specifically asked for twenty axes, ten shirts, sixteen mirrors, twelve scissors, one hundred nails, ten combs, one cast iron pot, one razor and one blanket. When these had been given, he looked around and pointed out a number of other articles he especially craved.

The natives were persistent in demanding presents. When the supplies of the missionaries ran low, and they ceased to give out gifts with a lavish hand, they were robbed of things they desperately needed, things which could not be replaced. Thievery was extremely common; in fact, it was a recognized part of Tahitian religion. One of their gods, Hiro, was the protector of thieves. When they went out to steal, Hiro was promised part of the booty in exchange for his assistance.

The missionaries discovered a class of people called Areois who had blackened their bodies with charcoal and dyed their faces red. They had no occupation other than dancing, boxing, wrestling and indulging in acts of buffoonery. They made it a practice to kill their children as soon as they were born. Iddeah, Pomare's wife, was a member of this society and had killed three of her children subsequent to the arrival of the missionaries.

Soon after reaching Tahiti on Sunday, March 19, 1797, Henry Nott and the missionary company conducted the first Christian service ever held on the shores of that dark island. The meeting was held under cover of some enormous trees. The king and a vast concourse of people were present. Pomare said he had been "dreaming about the Book of God which the missionaries had brought" and was eager to hear its message. What was the text used by the missionary speaker on this auspicious occasion? It was John 3:16, As its majestic syllables were translated by Peter, the Swede, and its momentous truths explained, Pomare nodded his head in approbation and exclaimed, "My ty! My ty! Very good! Very good!" And this sentiment was echoed by a host of dark-skinned savages.

"We are an ignorant people and this message is good for us," said the king.

"John 3:16 is the only sure and efficacious remedy for the ignorance and superstitions of mankind," said Henry Nott.

"My ty! Very good!" agreed the people.

II. JOHN 3:16 IS THE ONLY SURE AND EFFICACIOUS REMEDY FOR THE SORROWS OF MANKIND.

As the *Duff* sailed away on her mission to the Friendly and Marquesas Islands, the missionaries settled down to their new life among savages and with abounding enthusiasm, set about their divine mission. The Gospel of God's love in Christ held a mysterious attraction for the dark hearts of Tahiti. But little did they comprehend what transformations this Gospel demanded and was able to effect. The mercenary attitude of the people was indicated by their chief priest, Manne Manne, "You give me much talk and prayers, but very few axes, knives and scissors."

It would be difficult to exaggerate either the beauty of the island or the depravity of its inhabitants. A scene of unsurpassed beauty presented itself to the missionaries: the verdant valleys and stupendous mountains, the rich foliage of the breadfruit trees, the luxurious tropical pandanus, the waving plumes of lofty coconut groves, the exquisite lacery of enormous ferns, and, around it all, the white-crested pacific waters rolling waves of foam in splendid majesty upon the coral reefs, dashing its spray against the broken shore of such a scene: Bishop Heber wrote "Where every prospect pleases and only man is vile." The Tahitians wallowed in the abyss of sorrows into which the contaminations and corruptions of barbarism flowed.

The people were afflicted with the sorrows and desolations of war. A state of war was more normal than a state of peace, and there was a fearful destruction of life and property in their sanguinary conflicts. The houses of the defeated foe were burned, the prisoners were butchered in cold blood, and those who fled to the mountains were hunted down and slain like wild beasts. Oro was both the Mars and the Moloch of Polynesia. His altars were often stained with blood from human sacrifices offered to ensure his blessing in war or to appease his wrath.

The Tahitians were afflicted with the sorrows of cruelty and other abominations. In their wild longing for revenge, they would either openly pursue or secretly watch the object of their enmity as he went from place to place. When the enemy had at last been trapped and slain, the murderer, likely as not, would take a large stone and pound the body to pulp; then, having dried it in the sun, would cut a hole in the center, thrust his head through and wear it as a *tibuta* (Tahitian garment), the arms dangling in front and the legs in back.

A priest who officiated at one of the temples of Oro said to Nott, "When this temple was erected, every pillar which supports the roof was driven, like a stake, through the body of a human victim."

In his *Voyages*, Capt. Cook gave an accurate description of the Tahitian appearance and dress (or rather lack of it). But his estimate of their character was far too flattering. He did not remain with them long enough to fully discover the abominations which they practiced. It was commonplace to sacrifice children to their idols, to throw them into the sea to propitiate the sharks or to hurl them into the crater of a seething volcano as a sacred offering. Drunkenness was produced by a drink called kava, which caused the people to look and act more like demons than human beings.

When a man wished to atone for some crime he had committed, he would take to the sacred edifice a pig or fowl as an offering. If his crime was considered very serious, he would seek a human sacrifice. Pointing to a large tree, a native said to one of the missionaries, "Thousands of human sacrifices have hung from the branches of that one tree."

In the house of one of the chiefs there were many wooden gods, including those of the sun, moon, stars and sharks. Each had a sword, axe, or hammer in his hand. This, the priest said, was to be used to kill those who offended them unless an acceptable sacrifice was offered in atonement. Many cruelties were perpetrated upon the people as a part of their religion. By virtue of these offerings, the Tahitians were kept in a state of dire poverty. Nott says of a certain temple, "I saw offerings of whole hogs, turtles, large fish, plantains, coconuts, etc., all in a state of putrefaction and sending an offensive odor in all directions."

An idea of Tahitian barbarity may be formed from the dreadful weapons with which they slew one another. Among these was an instrument in the form of a long shaft, in which three spines from the tail of a rayfish were attached. These spines were strong, sharp bones, deeply barbed, and so artfully fastened, that, when struck into the body of an enemy, became instantly detached from the handle and remained rankling in the wound from which the barbs prevented their withdrawal. To be pierced by one of these meant certain death after days or weeks of excruciating torture.

The missionaries found that the population of Tahiti was only about one tenth the estimate Capt. Cook had made thirty years earlier. It may be that Capt. Cook's estimate was high, but it is certain that there had been a startling population decline. Two of the principal contributing factors were these:

1) the frightful licentiousness of the people.

2) the introduction of venereal and other diseases by the crews of foreign vessels.

Concerning the lechery of the Tahitians, Capt. Cook said, "There is an abyss of dissolute sensuality into which these people have sunk, wholly unknown to every other nation and which no imagination could possibly conceive." Henry Nott expressed the considered opinion that there was not in Tahiti a girl of twelve years who had escaped moral and physical contamination. In consequence, there was frightful suffering and the race was faced with extinction when the heralds of the Gospel arrived with their message of pardon, peace and purity.

Nott affirmed that two-thirds of all babies were killed at birth either by one of the parents or by one of those who were infant-killers by trade.

One of the monstrous practices of these islanders was to bury alive those whose infirmities made them a burden. They would dig a hole in the sand on the beach then, under pretense of taking the aged or sick relative to the sea to bathe, would take him to the spot, tumble him into the open grave, throw stones and earth upon him, trample the covering down with their feet and go away unconcerned. Then they would coolly share the spoil of property, which usually consisted of a few paltry articles.

It was among such a people that the missionaries began their apparently hopeless labors. Several of the unmarried men forsook the mission and married heathen women. One of them, Brother Lewis, was murdered a few months later. Several other missionaries went to Port Jackson and entered mercantile pursuits. Another, Brother Waters, went insane as he tried to teach the natives Hebrew and imagined himself in love with the queen. With heavy hearts the other missionaries continued their ministries of mercy and their efforts to master the language. In the early days they addressed the people instrumentally through Peter, the Swede, as interpreter. This was very unsatisfactory, since Peter was an extremely dissolute man and hostile to the objects of the mission. It was a day of rejoicing when, on August 10, 1801, the missionaries wrote the treasurer of the London Missionary Society, Mr. Hardcastle, stating: "We have the satisfaction of informing you that by the grace of God we hope, for the first time, publicly to address the natives on the next Lord's day. Brother Nott will be the speaker."

Henry Nott was only a bricklayer, but like William Carey in India, had marked linguistic abilities. He was the first to address the Tahitians publicly in their own tongue. As he faced the people on this auspicious day, with a rapturous gladness welling up in his soul, what was the message and text that fell from his lips? He said: "O Tahitians, I come with a message of infinite compassion to those in deep distress. I bring glad tidings of salvation to those in sin's control. I proclaim a Gospel of comfort to those in sorrow's gloom." Then he quoted the first verse he had translated into the Tahitian tongue—John 3:16.

A message of infinite compassion to those in deep distress!

Glad tidings of salvation to those in sin's control! A Gospel of comfort to those in sorrow's gloom! "God so loved the world."

III. JOHN 3:16 IS THE ONLY SURE AND EFFICACIOUS REMEDY FOR THE SINS OF MANKIND.

There were many things Henry Nott did not know, but he did know that his message was one of salvation, not of civilization. He knew that even if the savages could be civilized without being converted, their basic nature would remain unchanged and they would merely exchange the vices of barbarism for the vices of civilization. His message, therefore, was uncompromisingly evangelical and fervently evangelistic. But he was at great pains to make it clear that the regeneration wrought by the Spirit of God within must find expression in changed ethical and moral behavior without. It was chiefly this emphasis which aroused the natives' hostility. They were quite willing to become Christians in name, if only they could continue their heathen practices and be supplied with useful tools and novel toys from western countries.

There were many heartaches and many hardships for the valiant missionary band. Due to the Napoleonic Wars, four years elapsed without supplies or letters reaching them from England. During the ensuing seven years, supplies came only twice and, in one of these instances, had been ruined by salt water. The missionaries' shoes were completely worn out; their clothes all but rags. At times they could obtain food only by scouring the mountains for wild fruit. The *Duff* was captured by the French on its second missionary voyage in 1799, and all the twenty-nine missionary recruits, except one who died, returned to England.

The missionaries preached, prayed and did their utmost to bring King Pomare to a saving knowledge of Christ, but he died in 1803, a savage monster to the end. From the information obtainable, Nott estimated that, during his thirty-year reign, Pomare had sacrificed 2000 human victims as offerings to his idols. His son, Otu, assumed the title Pomare II. He was, if possible, more vicious and violent than his father. He committed so many acts of violence and incited the people to such hostility that, in 1805, after eight years of great suffering and of apparently fruitless endeavors, six of the missionaries removed from Tahiti to Huahine. Henry Nott was the moving spirit of the few who did not flee. He repeatedly went on long, arduous preaching tours. Having spent months and years over his lexicons, studying Hebrew and Greek, he translated the New and Old Testaments into the Tahitian language. As rapidly as possible the Word of Life was printed and distributed.

In 1808, the missionary house was destroyed; practically everything they owned had been stolen, and their printing type melted for bullets. Some missionaries fled then, others the following year. By the beginning of 1810 Henry Nott was all alone. He was "troubled...persecuted...cast down...but not in despair;" for he believed that the cause of Christ would one day triumph. Looking up at the majestic mountain called "The Diadem" he said: "That mountain is symbolic. It is a prophecy. This island will yet become a diadem of redeemed Tahitian jewels."

Prior to this, a group of brave English young women sailed for Tahiti to marry men they had never met and to make homes for them. One of these married Henry Nott and proved to be a worthy helpmate.

Nott one day quoted John 3:16 for possibly the thousandth time. A native exclaimed, "Is that true?"

Assured that it was, he replied: "Your God is unlike our gods. Your God has love; our gods have only cruelty. The offerings we make to them are only to propitiate them." Then he added sadly, "Your God has love for you but not for us wicked Tahitians."

Nott tenderly replied, "God's love in Christ extends to all. John 3:16 says, 'whosoever believeth.' That includes you." Henry Nott was convinced that any and every human heart could be won, if only made to realize that the wondrous love of God extends to him just as truly and completely as though no other soul existed on earth.

For many years Nott had given special attention to King Pomare II. Finally, his dark mind and savage heart began to respond to the message of John 3:16. He began to attend regular services held on the nearby island of Eimeo. With his help and encouragement, a chapel was built. It was dedicated July 25, 1813. During the ceremony of dedication, Nott announced that on the following day a meeting would be held for those who were ready to renounce idolatry and to learn about the service of the true God. Thirty-one natives responded, and a few days later, eleven others forsook their idols. The heathen called them "praying people." The number who renounced idolatry soon increased to about 800. Following a victorious battle on November 12, 1815, Pomare destroyed all the idols and altars he could find. The great idol Oro was first made a post for the king's kitchen and then cut up for firewood. Pomare took his own idols, twelve in number, to the missionaries and requested they be sent to the headquarters of the London Missionary Society. Schools were established in all parts of Tahiti; the abominations of heathenism were largely discontinued and thousands flocked to hear the sermons by Nott and his fellow workers, for by this time some of the missionaries who had fled to New Holland and New South Wales had returned. New recruits had also arrived.

Pomare provided the materials and erected a church at Papaoa, Tahiti, which measured 712 feet in length by 54 feet in breadth. It contained three pulpits, 260 feet apart; thus, three sermons were preached simultaneously. It was called the Royal Mission Chapel and was dedicated Tuesday, May 11, 1819. The following day Pomare promulgated a set of Christian laws by which the people were to regulate their conduct. Written by the bricklayer-missionary Henry Nott, they were the pattern for similar sets of laws adopted subsequently by Christian rulers on other Pacific islands.

Sunday, May 16, 1819, in the presence of 5000 people, King Pomare II was baptized. The contemporary account printed at the mission press in Tahiti two days later said: "Pomare was observed to lift up his eyes to heaven and move his lips in prayer. The sight was very moving, especially to our older brethren who had been watching over him for so many years."

Thus, after more than two decades of tears and toil, occurred the first baptism in Tahiti. After twenty-two years of hardships and disappointments, Henry Nott began to see the travail of his soul satisfied. In all the thrilling annals of missionary heroism, is there to be found anywhere a devotion to duty in the face of manifold perils, a fortitude under accumulated sufferings and a fidelity that held on so long with no evidence of harvest, to surpass that of the bricklayer of Tahiti?

The harvest was at last ready and the reapers were busy. During the ensuing decade hundreds of Tahitians were baptized and became eager students of God's Word and earnest seekers of souls. Some of them, and also some of the missionaries, went forth to take the Gospel to Borabora, Raiatea, Huahine and other dark islands. Nott preached in the huge Royal Mission Chapel on Sundays and Wednesdays and went on preaching tours through Tahiti and other islands. A building on Eimeo, formerly used for the offering up of human sacrifices and other abominable practices of the Areoi Society, was solemnly dedicated as a house of Christian worship. With 3000 people attending, Nott preached the dedication sermon using the test: "Thus saith the Lord, heaven is my throne and earth is my footstool."

During nearly 50 years of missionary service, Nott returned to his native land twice. Since only certain portions of the New Testament had been printed in Tahiti, he was eager to see the whole Tahitian Bible completed. This he accomplished during his second furlough from 1836 to 1838. While in England he had an interview with

Queen Victoria and presented her with a copy of his Bible. At her request, he read John 3:16 in Tahitian.

Returning to Tahiti, he labored on. May 1, 1844, he heard the Master summon and went Home. One of his colleagues, Joseph Moore, wrote, "During his last days he conversed much on the great subject of salvation."

When the books at God's right hand are opened, it will be revealed that some of the noblest "Giants of Faith" were men who, with only the rudiments of a formal education, lived lives that were yielded truly to Christ and wielded mightily in His service. High on the Roll of Honor will be the following:

1. William Carey, the consecrated cobbler, who stirred a sleeping church to action and labored so valiantly in India.

2. Alexander Mackay, the consecrated mechanic, who endured such tears and toils in banishing the darkness of Uganda.

3. Henry Nott, the consecrated bricklayer, who, by his heroic sufferings and unwearied labors, opened the doors of Tahiti and Polynesia to the sublime tidings of a matchless text: "For God so loved the world, that he gave his only begotten Son, that whosoever believeth in him should not perish, but have everlasting life."

HENRY NOTT

QUESTIONS, TOPICS, AND ASSIGNMENTS
FOR STUDY

1. How is Henry Nott's life text woven into the story of his life?

2. What did Martin Luther call the "little gospel"? Do you see any comparison between this text and the reformation text, "The just shall live by faith"?

3. How many years was Henry Nott in Tahiti without a single conversion for the Lord? What does this incident tell us about Henry Nott's personality and convictions?

4. Was there any single factor that kept the heathen from believing? If so, what was it?

5. What part did William Carey play in the establishment of a mission on Tahiti?

6. Outline the religious superstitions of the people of Tahiti. Cambridge, University Press—*Religious and Social Organization in Central Polynesia*, 1937. Cambridge, University Press—*Religious and Cosmic Beliefs of Central Polynesia*, 1933 (2 volumes).

7. What strikes you as being odd about the two sailors that were on Tahiti? Can you connect this with Biblical characters?

8. What was the natives' concept of missions and the missionary's message? How did Nott overcome this with his approach and message? How did the natives react before and after?

9. How can we understand people by observing their lives, economy, morals, etc.?

10. Were the natives aware of their sins? What do you notice about the sacrifices?

11. Why are the words, *pardon, peace* and *purity* applied to the Gospel message especially applicable?

12. Are there problems on the mission field among the missionaries? If so, what are they? Use Tahiti as an example.

13. Write a paragraph on your impressions of the testimony of Henry Nott.

14. From the natives' point of view, what was the chief difference between their gods and our God and why? Can you compare other non-Christian faiths in this respect? Explain.

15. List the things that the Lord accomplished through Henry Nott.

16. How many years did Henry Nott serve the Lord on the mission field? What would you attribute to his success?

17. What is so significant about the occupations of these missionaries? What qualifications does the Lord set for a missionary? Can the Lord use anyone?

18. What have you been able to apply to your own life from the dedicated life of Henry Nott?

ADDITIONAL READINGS ON HENRY NOTT

Encyclopaedia Americana

Encyclopaedia Britannica

The New International Encyclopaedia

These have information on the Society Islands and Tahiti:

James hall and Charles Nordhoff—*Faery Land of the South Sea.* "Tahitian Tales" is a chapter on folklore, giving you a greater concept of the people and their thoughts (pp. 303-317).

Hawthorne Daniel—*Islands of the Pacific*, pp. 42-58, 1943. Provides an overall view of the island in reference to geographical location, terrain, etc.

Gifford Pinchot—*To the South Seas*, 1930, pp. 476-492. The cruise of the schooner *Mary Pinchott* in the South Sea Islands including Tahiti.

John Ritchie—*Oceania's Shores*, pp. 18-22. The story of how the Gospel was carried to the New Zealand Aborigines and the South Sea Island cannibals.

Richard Lovett—*History of the London Missionary Society* London Missionary Society—*A Missionary Voyage to the Southern Pacific Ocean*, published in London in 1799. An extremely interesting original source for material on the establishment of the mission in Tahiti. For the thrilling story of Captain James Wilson's odyssey while on board the *Duff*, and for further information concerning the early years of the Tahiti mission, see Eugene M. Harrison—*Blazing the Missionary Trail*, pp. 7-20, published by Van Kampen Press, Wheaton, Illinois.

WILLIAM CAREY

THE COBBLER WHO TURNED DISCOVERER
(1761 – 1834)

One Sunday morning, in the month of December, 1829, the missionary's prayer time, preparatory to the preaching service, was interrupted by the arrival of an official messenger from Lord Bentinck of Calcutta. The document bore stupendous import, namely, the banishment by legal enactment of the practice of Sati —one of the most horrible of all the depravities of heathenism. For more than 35 years the missionary had raised his voice in fervent protest against the monstrous cruelties involved in the custom of burning Indian widows in order that they might go into the spirit-land to continue serving their husbands—a practice resulting each year in the burning of thousands. Most appropriately, the one who exerted the greatest influence in stirring up the Christian conscience against suttee (Sati), both in India and England, was asked to translate the decree embodying its abolishment into Bengali.

Quickly arranging with another to lead the service and preach, the overjoyed missionary took the official document and turned again to his prayer closet. Opening his Bible at his favorite passage, Isaiah 54, he mingled Scripture reading and prayer in an ecstasy of thanksgiving. Turning to the task at hand, he spent the rest of the day making a careful translation of the historic document. Again, at sun down, he turned to Isaiah 54 and to prayer. After reading aloud from verse five, "Thy Redeemer...shall be called the God of the whole earth," and then verses eleven and thirteen, he prayed: "I thank Thee, Father, for this surpassingly sweet promise which Thou didst vouchsafe to me long ago, with its assurance of the ultimate banishment of all heathen devices and abominations, and of the ultimate winning of all hearts to Thy allegiance. Use even Thine unworthy servant to speed the day of fulfillment, the day when all the benighted sons of men shall become Thy people and all the kingdoms of this world shall become the kingdoms of Thy dear Son."

This man, with continents and empires upon his brain, was William Carey, a maker of shoes and a maker of history with a history-making text embedded in his soul: "Thy Redeemer...shall be called the God of the whole earth."

Who? "Thy REDEEMER."

Whose Redeemer? "THY Redeemer."

Is the promise assured? "Thy Redeemer SHALL BE CALLED."

Is the promise limited? "...THE WHOLE EARTH."

What is the promise? "*Thy Redeemer shall be called the God of the whole earth.*"

Historians agree this man was one of the giants of Christian history.

George Adam Smith asserts, "It is no exaggeration to call Carey one of the greatest of God's Englishmen."

A.T. Pierson says of Carey, "With little teaching, he became learned. Poor himself, he made millions rich. By birth obscure, he rose to unsought eminence. And seeking only to follow the Lord's leading, he led forward the Lord's hosts."

"The Christian Church," according to J.D. Freeman, "owes more to William Carey and his mission than to any other man or movement since the days of Paul. He gave her a new horizon, kindled within her a new life and soul. Upon the trellis of the mission enterprise, the Church's vine has run over the wall. It has given her a southern exposure, through which she has felt at her heart the thrill of a new vitality, while bearing on her outmost branches a burden of precious fruit for the vintage of the skies."

William Carey was born in Paulers Pury, England, August 17, 1761. Early he evidenced a singular interest in natural history. He made frequent excursions into the woods and across the fields, always on the alert to discover and identify a new bird, animal or plant, He was thrilled by tales of adventure, especially those associated with the magic name of the man who, sailing west, discovered a vast new world in 1492, accounting for the reason his companions nicknamed him "Columbus." Little did they imagine that he would become greater than Columbus, a discoverer of worlds which seem to have eluded the famous Italian, an adventurer who crossed the seas, not seeking to dispossess others of their gold, but to distribute —as lavishly as possible—"the unsearchable riches of Christ."

I. THE COBBLER DISCOVERS THE REDEEMER

The first words of Carey's great text are, "Thy Redeemer." Until he had met the Redeemer face to face and found out the merits of His grace, these words could have no reference to him. No discovery of consequence is possible until this discovery has been made.

Approaching the age of 17, realizing that it was high time to choose a trade, Carey turned to shoemaking. His father was not able to provide the accustomed payment for a seven-year apprenticeship. He sought, therefore, a man who would provide him with work while learning the trade. This led to the selection of Clarke Nichols of Piddington: this particular gentleman having the additional qualification of being a reputable and strict churchman—an important factor in the eyes of Carey's father. Although young Carey learned much about the shoemaking business, his new employer's influence was far from wholesome. The young apprentice was actually driven away from Christ and the Church by his association with Nichols, chiefly because of his fiery temper, profane tongue and Saturday night drinking sprees.

Carey's co-apprentice was John Warr, a devout, young dissenter or non-conformist; that is, one who dissented from, and refused to conform to the practices of the state church, the Church of England. Dissenters were often penalized and persecuted due to their refusal to attend the established church and their insistence upon having churches of their own wherein they might worship according to their understanding of God's Word and of God's will. John Warr's soul was exercised for the salvation of his fellow apprentice. "He became importunate with me," says Carey, "lending me books and engaging in conversation with me whenever possible." But Carey's heart was both hard and proud. He said later, "I had pride sufficient for a thousand times my knowledge. I always scorned to have the worst in discussion and the last word was assuredly mine. But I was often afterward convinced that my fellow apprentice had the better of the argument, and I felt a growing uneasiness, but had no idea that nothing but a complete change of heart could do me any good."

His experience was similar to that of David Brainerd and Martin Luther who, under conviction, saw that the root of their trouble lay *in the heart*.

"*I had a very good outside, but my heart was exceedingly sinful,*" said Brainerd.

"*My austerities did not change my heart,*" said Luther.

"*My heart was hard and proud,*" said Carey. "*Nothing but a change of heart could do me any good.*"

Impressed not only by Warr's concern on his behalf but also by the spiritual beauty of his life, Carey agreed to attend some of the services at the Dissenters Church where the Word of God was preached with the warmth and demonstration of the Spirit. Eventually he was brought under deep conviction and, at the age of 17, was ready to exchange the pharisee's self-righteousness for the publican's penitence and submission. Like Pilgrim, he entered the wicket Gate and set out for the Heavenly City. When John Warr led this lad to Christ, he had no idea he was winning the one who would sound the call of God to a sleeping church and add the jewel of India to the diadem of Christ.

Carey had experienced the inexpressible wonders of the New Birth. The Redeemer of "the whole earth" was now his Redeemer. The lad nicknamed "Columbus" had made a discovery of greater present and eternal import than the discovery of a new continent or an unknown sea. And having made this discovery, there would be no end to the discoveries that would break, with sunrise glory, upon his redeemed and adventuresome spirit.

The eminent scientist and inventor, Lord Kelvin, was once asked, "What is the greatest discovery you ever made?" His reply was, "The discovery of Jesus Christ as my Saviour and Lord." When another was asked the same question, he replied, "My greatest discovery was to find out how great a sinner I am and how great a Saviour is Christ." William Carey, the cobbler who turned discoverer, was of very much the same mind.

II. THE COBBLER DISCOVERS THE JOY OF JOINING THE REDEEMER IN QUEST OF SOULS

In his beloved Isaiah, Carey found many references to "joy" and "singing." Two such references are to be found in the first verse of his favorite chapter, Isaiah 54. The thought is: "You are no longer estranged from God. Your heart is no longer desolate and barren.

Therefore, sing!" The joy of knowing the Redeemer melts into the joy of sharing the Redeemer's passion and purpose, as set forth in the verses that follow.

Having tasted the sweetness and wonder of redeeming grace, Carey became concerned for his master and others whose lives gave such evidence of the need of regeneration and of new life in Christ. At first Clarke Nichols was obdurate; then, he became ill, smitten down with a fatal malady. John Warr and William Carey found him at last humble and willing to listen as they read from God's Word, "He that heareth…and believeth…is passed from death unto life." Thus his death chamber was transformed into the birthplace of his immortal soul, and Carey entered the radiant ranks of those whose preeminent joy is "to seek and to save the lost."

Have a good look at the scene in Clarke Nichols' death chamber.

The *bed* speaks of death!

The *Book* speaks of *life*!

"He that believeth is passed from death unto life."

At the age of 19, Carey fell in love with Dorothy Plackett, and they were married June 10, 1781. She was a faithful and devoted wife, though she fell far behind Carey in spiritual discernment and never shared his great missionary passion.

Immediately upon his conversion, Carey became an ardent student of the Scriptures. Eager to know exactly and fully what the Scriptures taught, he began an earnest study of the original Hebrew and Greek languages of Scripture. His aptness and earnestness in discourse soon became known, and was asked at various times and places to expound the Word. Having transferred his residence to Moulton, where he opened a school, he was asked by a small company of Baptists to be their pastor. The salary was about $50.00

per year. His chief support for his family came from his earnings as a cobbler and as a schoolteacher. Several years later (1789) he moved to Leicester to serve as pastor of the Harvey Lane Baptist Church. He found the church in a state of disunion, dishonor and spiritual impotence, largely due to worldliness and resultant evils among the members. He prayed and preached most fervently, but conversions were impossible in such an atmosphere, and the pastor was heartbroken. Eventually, in September , 1790, he determined upon a bold course of procedure—one that many twentieth century churches could follow to great advantage. He proposed that the church membership be dissolved, that a solemn covenant embodying New Testament faith, life and discipline be prepared, and that only those accepting this covenant be accepted as members of the newly-constituted church. This was done, the church was revived, worldly nettles gave place to the fruitage of the Spirit, and in response to the preaching from the pulpit and witnessing in the homes, were many blessed conversions. He led his sisters, his wife and many others into the sublime experience of redemption. In his zeal for souls, he frequently made preaching trips to surrounding villages, laying the foundations for a number of churches.

Carey was now a radiantly happy man. He had entered into the joy of the Good Shepherd in bringing home the lost sheep. His heart was vibrant with the ecstasy which causes all heaven to rejoice "over one sinner that repenteth." He could "sing" and "break forth into singing" (Isaiah 54:1) in the celestial joy of sharing with others the mystic merit of the Redeemer's love.

III. THE COBBLER DISCOVERS THAT THE REDEEMER'S CONCERN AND THE CHURCH'S RESPONSIBILITY ARE WORLD-WIDE

The cattle, in the quiet of the early morning Northamptonshire pasture, were disturbed by the sound of footsteps in the lane. Turning their gaze in the direction of the sounds, the cattle saw a familiar figure and continued their grazing. The figure was the village cobbler carrying a load of newly made shoes to market. He was oblivious of the cattle and even of the loveliness of nature in her summer gown. His thoughts were far, far away. Walking, he said to himself, "Surely God means what He says. Surely He means for us who know Him to carry the message of redemption to all men everywhere."

Without a doubt, God means what He says!

When He says "GO," He means "GO!"

When He says "Go YE," He means "Go YE!"

When He says "INTO ALL THE WORLD," He means "INTO ALL THE WORLD!"

When He says "PREACH THE GOSPEL," He means "PREACH THE GOSPEL!"

When He says "Go...TO EVERY CREATURE," He means "TO EVERY CREATURE!"

Surely God means what He says!

With love for Christ burning in his soul, Carey kept reading and rereading Isaiah 54:5, "Thy Redeemer...shall be called the God of the whole earth." He also read in the New Testament of Christ's compassion for the lost sheep of all nations and of His command to preach the Gospel to all the world. At a ministers' meeting he proposed they consider "whether the command given to the Apostles to evangelize all nations is not binding on all succeeding ministers to the end of the world, seeing that the accompanying promise is of equal extent."

The command is, "Go and make disciples of all nations."

The promise is, "Lo, I am with you." Has anyone the right to play leapfrog with the command and then hug the promise?

J.C. Ryland was merely expressing the universal attitude of the Church when he impatiently interrupted Carey and exclaimed, "Sit down, young man, sit down and be still. When God wants to convert the heathen, He will do it without consulting either you or me." Carey sat down, but a vision of faraway lands and of multitudes in darkness haunted his soul, and he could not be still. In and out of season, in conversation and in sermon, he dealt with one all-absorbing theme, namely, the responsibility of the Church to launch out upon its long-neglected, world-wide mission. For eight years he devoted his spare time to making maps of heathen lands and gathering data as to their location, size, population and religions, and studying the arguments supporting the view that the missionary enterprise is the Church's highest and holiest endeavor. He incorporated these years of research and thought into a lengthy pamphlet entitled "The Enquiry." After picturing the desperate condition of the world where Christ was not known and enthroned, he put the trumpet of God to his lips and sounded the divine call to action. He closed with an appeal for persistent prayer, bold planning and sacrificial giving. Citing his three beloved heroes, he stated,

> *What a treasure, what a harvest must await such as Paul and Eliot and Brainerd, who have given themselves wholly to God's work! What a heaven to see the myriads of the heathen who by their labours have been brought into the knowledge of God! Surely it is worthwhile to lay ourselves out with all our might in promoting Christ's Kingdom!*

The next episode in Carey's missionary crusade was his deathless sermon at Nottingham, May 31, 1792. The occasion was the annual meeting of the Baptist churches of that district. Carey was to preach the opening sermon. As he rose to speak that historic morning, the woe and misery of an anguished world surged through the channels of a single heart. He turned the searchlight upon two mighty truths of Scripture, particularly as enunciated in Isaiah 54. First, the Redeemer's saving concern is as wide as humanity. "Thy Redeemer...shall be called the God of the whole earth." Second, the Redeemer's concern and the Church's responsibility are coextensive. When God says "Thy Redeemer," He is speaking to the Church and, therefore, to every individual Christian. Spending most of his time on this second point, the cobbler-preacher rang out the challenge of God found in verses 2 and 3 of Isaiah 54: "Enlarge the place of thy tent, and stretch forth the curtains of thine habitations...lengthen thy cords and strengthen thy stakes... thy seed shall inherit the nations and make the desolate places to be inhabited." Carey was convinced that God was saying to the Church: "Rouse up from your complacency. Find larger canvas, stouter and taller tent poles, stronger tent pegs. Catch wider visions. Dare bolder programs. Rouse up and go forth to conquer for Christ even the uttermost parts and the isles of the sea."

Carey's soul was captivated by an epochal discovery. In consequence, he was dreaming of continents and empires to be brought under the sway of Christ. He was thinking, not just of England or of Europe, but of the world. How the familiar scriptural expression burned in his soul!

"God so loved *the world!*"

"Go ye into all *the world!*"

"Christ, the Saviour of *the world!*"

"God in Christ reconciling *the world!*"

"A propitiation for the sins of *the world!*"

"Thy Redeemer...the God of *the whole world!*"

All the passion of the inspired preacher's heart poured out in two stupendous exhortations:

"Expect great things from God!"

"Attempt great things for God!"

Concerning the message, Dr. Ryland said:

> *If all the people had lifted up their voices and wept, as the Children of Israel did at Bochim, I should not have wondered at the effect; it would only have seemed proportionate to the cause, so clearly did Mr. Carey prove the criminality of our supineness in the cause of God!*

But alas! the people did not weep! They did not even pause to pray! To them it was just another sermon, nice to listen to, but not to be taken too seriously. When Carey saw the people rising to leave as usual, he seized Andrew Fuller's hand and exclaimed in an agony of distress, "Are we not going to do anything? Oh, Fuller, call them back and let's do something in answer to God's call!

That was a portentous moment in the history of Christ's redemptive purpose. Deep called unto deep. Fuller, too, heard "God's sigh in the heart of the world" and joined with Carey in demanding action. Before the meetings closed, a motion was passed to this effect: "Resolved, that a plan be prepared against the next Ministers' Meeting at Kettering, for forming a Baptist society for propagating the Gospel among the heathen."

Expecting great things from God, William Carey inspired others to join him in attempting great things for God.

This marks the birth of the modern missionary movement, which, during the succeeding century and a half, has sent many tens of thousands of consecrated heralds of the cross "into all the world" with a message of redemption and of social transformation through Christ.

IV. THE COBBLER DISCOVERS THAT THE REDEEMER IS CALLING HIM TO FOREIGN SERVICE

Several months after the Nottingham meetings, the proposed missionary society was formed. Subscriptions amounting to about $65.00 were taken, and the group of subscribers looked around for missionaries, as well as for additional donors. They had also to decide in what field to commence their missionary efforts. Their attention was forcibly directed toward India by contact with a Mr. Thomas who had returned to England after spending several years in India as a surgeon. He had also put forth considerable effort to spread the Gospel, and he had a stirring story to tell of conditions and missionary opportunities in India.

In the light of developing events, Carey kept asking the question, "What is now my part in this expanding enterprise?" With a wife and three children to support, should he not continue to shepherd the church now thriving at Leicester and to stir up missionary concern throughout England? Or did God desire him to become the leader of the overseas mission which he had so urged upon his brethren? Turning again to Isaiah 54, he discovered six startling words which immediately followed and indeed were a part of his great text: "For the Lord hath called thee." The Holy Spirit confirmed in his soul that these words did constitute the divine call to him to cross the seas as a witness of the Redeemer's concern for a lost world. The cobbler—turned—discoverer had made some phenomenal discoveries, but none more significant than this. This "Columbus" was now highly resolved to sail the seas to discover and claim for his Lord a vast new world of infinitely precious souls.

When Andrew Fuller, secretary of the newly formed missionary society, read the account given by Mr. Thomas of conditions and

Gospel opportunities in India, he remarked how there was a gold mine in India, but it seemed almost deep as the center of the earth. "Who will venture to explore it?" he asked. Carey was quick to reply, "I will venture to go down, but remember that you—you who remain at home—must hold the ropes." And by "holding the ropes" he was referring to the support of prayer and heart concern, even more than of money. His offer was gladly accepted by the Society. He and Thomas were appointed. But when his wife heard of it, she refused to accompany him. Carey was very devoted to his family, but his supreme devotion was to Him who said, "If any man love father or mother or wife more than me, he is not worthy of me." He made suitable arrangements for the support of his family, preached to his sorrowing congregation a farewell message on the Great Commission, and he and Thomas set out to raise funds and secure a passage to India. There were many disappointments and protracted delays. Meanwhile, Mrs. Carey gave birth to her fifth child. One child having died, she now had four living children under nine years of age. Definite sailing arrangements were finally made. Carey, accompanied by Thomas, hurried home to make a final plea to his wife to accompany him. Let it be stated as "an everlasting memorial of her" that, on a single day's notice and with a baby not yet a month old, she consented to go on condition that her sister, Kitty, should go along as companion and helper. Thus, when Carey finally embarked for India, his wife, children, Kitty and Thomas were on board with him.

William Carey was a missionary trailblazer. As his holy enthusiasm spread, other missionary societies formed in rapid succession. Besides those on the continent and in America, by 1834 there were 14 societies in Britain, the Baptist being the first. As Greenough has stated:

> *The light, which Carey kindled, spread from hill to hill like beacon fires, till every Christian church in turn recognized the signal and responded to the call. The consecrated cobbler was indeed 'the Father of Modern Missions.'*

Carey deserves to rank among the noblest and best of England's immortal great, not only because of the incalculable boon to India and to the world of the missionary movement he launched, but also because that movement saved England's own soul. Englishmen first went to India to gain wealth as merchants then to gain land as soldiers and adventurers. But with the coming of Carey and the emergence of a missionary passion, England began to feel that her true greatness was to be realized not in economic or military conquest, but in giving to India "a Saviour, which is Christ the Lord."

What shall profit a nation if it gains a vast empire, yet loses its own soul?

What shall profit people if they send ships of commerce to the seven seas yet suffer the shipwreck of their faith?

V. THE COBBLER DISCOVERS THAT THE REDEEMER'S BLESSING IS UPON HIS FAITHFUL WITNESSES

After a tempestuous journey of five months during which Carey made a diligent study of Bengali, the party reached Calcutta on Nov. 11, 1793. His first impressions served only to accentuate his heart's distress over India's need. Like Paul at Athens, he was moved by the people's deep-seated religious nature as expressed by the innumerable shrines, the offerings of food, flowers and the incredible sufferings they readily endured in their quest for spiritual peace. With anguished soul, he saw Indian devotees lying on beds of spikes, walking on spiked shoes, swinging themselves on flesh hooks, gazing at the sun until they lost their sight and, in manifold ways, inflicting torture upon their bodies. Most terrible of all was the practice of suttee widow burning. Against this barbaric custom Carey threw the weight of his utmost energy, until, as related earlier, it was finally abolished by legal action in 1829.

Carey's expectations of success in the mission were at first very sanguine. He felt assured that soon as he could converse freely in the vernacular, he would be able to lead large numbers "out of darkness into His marvelous light." But months lengthened into years without a single convert. This failure led frequently to tears and bitter self-reproach. Carey did not attempt to satisfy his qualms of conscience by imagining that his physical presence in a foreign land made him a missionary. He had come to India to win lost, wretched souls to Christ and nothing could compensate the failure toward this endeavor. At times his faith became faint, but always rallied through the recurrence of "the blessed hour of prayer." Several times his eager hopes were crushed by the dismal failure and lapse into idolatry on the part of some for whose conversion he had long labored. In the hour of midnight discouragement, he turned to his treasured Isaiah 54. As he read, "Thou shalt not be ashamed...Thy Redeemer shall be called the God of the whole earth," he discovered the note of certitude, and leaning heavily on the divine faithfulness, kept on "expecting great things."

How abounding was his joy when, after seven long years of travail of soul, he and Thomas found a convert ready to endure afflictions and to be publicly baptized. This was Krishna Pal, whose devotion to Christ found expression in these tender lines which later became part of a frequently used hymn:

> *O thou, my soul, forget no more,*
> *The Friend who all thy sorrows bore.*
> *Let every idol be forgot.*
> *But, O my soul, forget Him not.*

Carey's cup of joy filled up and overflowed that blessed Sunday, Dec. 28, 1800, when he was privileged to baptize his own son, Felix, and then Krishna Pal. Poor Thomas was so overwhelmed with joy that historic morning—"Sing, soul, sing!" he exclaimed,

"Sing aloud! Unutterable is my gladness!"—that his mind was temporarily deranged and he was unable to attend the baptismal service.

Christ set them in the ecstasy
Of His great jubilee;
He gave them dancing heart and shining face,
And lips filled full of grace
And pleasure, as the rivers and the sea.

After all, Krishna Pal was only one. Why so great exultation?

Krishna Pal was only one, but was not one lost sheep esteemed of great value by the shepherd?

Krishna Pal was only one, but how diligently the shepherd sought the one lost sheep and how joyously he brought it home!

Krishna Pal was only one, but the angels in heaven took note and rejoiced together around the throne!

Krishna Pal was only one, but a continent was coming after him!

Prior to this signal event, Carey's heart had been tremendously encouraged by the coming of consecrated helpers, notably Marshman and Ward, and the moving of the mission to Serampore, which was in the territory held by the Danes where they had greater protection and freedom of activity than in the confines of the East India Company.

There were, for Carey, many joys and many sorrows. Among the latter was the death of his five-year-old son, Peter. His heaviest cross was the condition of his wife, who became deranged in mind and continued in this state until her death in December, 1807. The following year he was married to a Danish lady, Charlotte Rumohr, who had been baptized in 1801—the first European lady to bear this witness in India—and had shown exceptional zeal for the evangelization of the Indians. Despite her frailty of health, she was a true helpmate for Carey. Her spirituality, her intimate knowledge of Danish, Italian, French, and her delight in the study of Scripture in these three versions, made her his invaluable companion in Biblical translating. She had "a soul of fire in a shell of pearl." She passed away in 1821. In 1823 Carey married Grace Hughes, who became a devoted helpmate.

Carey experienced severe sorrow when his son, Felix, turned from missionary labors to become a special government agent in Burma. Writing to England he sadly stated: "My son has chosen to be an ambassador of the King of England when he might have risen to the status of being an ambassador of the King of Kings."

Carey had exceptional linguistic gifts. With assiduity and remarkable success, he devoted himself to the study of Sanskrit, Bengali, Hindustani and other native tongues. His excellence in this field made it possible for him to become Professor of Sanskrit and Bengali in Fort William College, Calcutta, at a salary of 500 rupees a month. It is an evidence of his selflessness that he devoted his entire salary to the work of spreading the Gospel, keeping only a small portion for necessary expenses. As Carey stated, "We might have had large possessions, but we have given all to the mission."

For 41 years Carey was the recognized leader of the growing Indian mission. Never in Christian history has there appeared a man with greater versatility of gifts or consecration more complete. He was India's pioneer in agriculture, horticulture and in the promotion of vernacular education. He was the moving spirit of the Serampore Trio who set up and operated the first steam engine in India, introduced the large scale manufacture of paper, inaugurated the printing industry by the establishment of the great Mission Press, and built a college which still stands to train Christian leaders to engage in the conquest of India for Christ. He was interested in social reform as an expression of the Christian spirit, and used his influence against suttee and the practice of casting babies into the Ganges as a sacrifice to the gods. It was Carey who founded the Christian Church in India. Incredible as it seems, it was this same erstwhile cobbler who, with the help of associates, translated and printed the Word of God—either the whole or the most precious parts thereof—into 34 different tongues. In the book of Revelation, John tells of seeing an angel who gained authority over the nations, not by the might of armies, navies, and airplanes, but by the power of a Book that was "open in his hand." It was the privilege of Carey and his associates to put this incomparable Book into the hands of India's millions and to open its matchless message to their wondering hearts.

VI. THE SECRET OF THE COBBLER'S SUCCESS

Where shall we turn to find the secret of a life so remarkable? What are the causes adequate to explain such stupendous achievements? The basic answer is to be found in the recognition that Carey was a veritable "Columbus." What he was and what he did are to be computed—not in terms of achievements—but as discoveries. He did not achieve his salvation; he discovered it, as a pearl of great price, a treasure of the field. His so-called achievements were but the out-working of the fragrance and power of the indwelling Redeemer. His virtues and qualities of greatness were but the fruitage of "constantly abiding" in the Vine. Just as the branch might say of the grape clusters that hang thereon, "It is not of me!" so the Christian says of success, "It is not of me! It is the vintage of abiding in my abounding Lord."

Much in Carey's career finds its explanation in *his unconquerable persistence*. His sister, Mary, said: "Whatever he begins, he finishes." This trait is illustrated by an incident of his youth, related with accustomed felicity by Dr. Boreham. In his eager quest for knowledge of wild life of every sort, young Carey climbed a tall chestnut tree in search of a coveted bird's nest. Before reaching it, he slipped and fell. Again he tried and failed. On the third attempt he fell and broke his leg. A few weeks later, the limb still bandaged, he slipped away and returned with the nest.

"You don't mean to tell me that you climbed that tree again!" exclaimed his mother.

"I couldn't help it, mother," he replied. "Really, I couldn't. When I begin a thing, I must go through with it!"

Carey himself said that whatever success attended his efforts in India was due to the fact that he was a plodder. Having begun a great work for God, having put his hand to the plow, nothing could cause him to let go or look back.

Carey was a man of amazing faith. He did not expect financial support beyond passage money to India. Whatever came, either from the homeland or from his stipend as professor, was turned into the general funds of the mission. He believed implicitly that the Lord who sent him would supply him. By faith he set out for "a place which he was to receive as an inheritance," being responsible for the support of seven souls. By faith he turned his face away from the homeland, never to return, and "sojourned in a strange land" for 40 years. By faith he overcame a multitude of adversaries and presented unto God "a more excellent sacrifice" whereby "he being dead yet speaketh." By faith he foresaw the day when the Gospel of Christ would relegate Krishna, Kali and Siva to the oblivion into which it had swept Jupiter and Venus and Isis long ago.

Nothing was more characteristic of Carey than his consuming concern for souls. This zeal constantly manifested itself while he was still in England. When a neighbor remonstrated with him for spending so much time preaching, to the neglect of his shoe business, he replied, "My real business is to preach the Gospel and win lost souls. I cobble shoes to pay expenses." More than once the pupils in his school saw their teacher burst into tears, as during a geography lesson when he pointed to a world map or to a globe he had made with odd pieces of leather exclaiming, "The people living in these areas are pagans! They are lost, hundreds of millions of them, not knowing the blessed Saviour!" Whether in England or India, Carey had a hot heart for souls. His heart was hot with gladness over the converted and hot with compassion over the unreached.

A hot heart for souls!

The surest expression of a redeemed spirit!

The indispensable qualification of a missionary!

The transcendent attribute of those whom heaven calls great!

His humility and the sweetness of his devotion to Christ stand out in Carey's life from the time of his conversion until his coronation. In a letter to Dr. Ryland, January 30, 1823, he writes, "I have long made the language of Psalm 51 my own – 'Have mercy upon me, O God…according unto the multitude of thy tender mercies blot out my transgressions.' Should you outlive me, and have any influence to prevent it, I earnestly request that no epithets of praise may ever accompany my name. All such expressions would convey a falsehood. To me belong shame and confusion of face. I can only say, 'Hangs my helpless soul on Thee.'"

During his last illness, Carey said to Alexander Duff, "Mr. Duff, you have been saying much about Dr. Carey and his work. After I am gone, please speak not of Dr. Carey, but rather of my wonderful Saviour."

By Carey's explicit instruction his grave marker was to contain nothing more than his name, the dates of his birth, death, and two lines from Isaac Watts, his favorite hymn writer:

A wretched, poor and helpless worm,
On Thy kind arms I fall.

His soul was set for its final voyage and its last great discovery. At sunrise, June 9, 1834, William Carey discovered the unimagined and inexpressible glories which the Redeemer had in store for His own. He entered into "the heritage of the servants of the Lord" and into the fulfillment of the promise of Isaiah 54:8, "With everlasting kindness will I have mercy on thee, saith the Lord the Redeemer."

While honoring the memory of the consecrated cobbler who was so mightily used of God, let it be remembered that Christ is still in urgent need of heralds of His redemptive passion, and that it is the incomparable privilege of every saved and surrendered soul to be a discoverer of new worlds to be won in the Redeemer's name.

WILLIAM CAREY

QUESTIONS, TOPICS, AND ASSIGNMENTS
FOR STUDY

1. What was William Carey's great text? Write it out in your notebook in bold letters, as on a placard.

2. Note carefully Carey's mental preparation

    A. As a boy
    B. As a young man after his conversion

S. Pearce Carey—*William Carey*, pp. 4-54
George Smith—*Life of William Carey*, pp. 1-19

3. Observe the expository manner in which the author uses the salient ideas of the text as the basis for the formulation of the main divisions of the chapter and weaves all the materials into a pattern of unity around the person's life text.

4. Note the influences that led Carey to make the supreme discovery of life.

5. In what respect was the experience of Brainerd, Luther and Carey alike?

6. Study carefully Carey's "Enquiry"—as to the effort put into its composition, as to the common objections to missionary endeavors which he turned to arguments for missions, etc.

George Smith—*William Carey*, pp. 24–28
S. Pearce Carey—*William Carey*, pp. 68–77

7. Would the drastic action of Carey, relative to the Baptist church in Leicester, be advantageous in some churches today?

8. What type of theology dominated the thinking of most Christians of Carey's day? Include J.C. Ryland. What caused Ryland to say "When God wants to convert the heathen, He will do it without consulting either you or me?" In this connection, read Romans 8:29 and S. Pearce Carey's book, p. 88.

9. Who was "the Widow Wallis?" Note the connection between Nottingham and Kettering. Catch the drama in Carey's Nottingham sermon, its seeming failure, etc.

10. Was Carey a soul winner before going to India? Cite examples.

11. As to Mrs. Carey:

    A. Was she qualified mentally and spiritually to enter into her husband's labors?
    B. Why did she at first refuse to accompany her husband to India?
    C. What was her mental condition in India? See Smith, pp. 134–135.

12. Do you see any evidence of divine providence and guidance in the fact that Carey went to India instead of to Tahiti? How?

13. Give, succinctly, several reasons why Carey is called "the founder" or "father of modern missions."

14. What was suttee (or sati)? Name other debasing practices encountered by Carey in India. Did they exist in spite of the religion of the people or as an integral part of it?

15. Who was Krishna Pal? Note his significance. What happened to Dr. Thomas that historic day, Dec. 28, 1800?

16. What did Carey do with his salary as professor in Fort William College?

17. Who constituted the famous "Serampore Trio?" What was the work of each?

18. Briefly outline Carey's monumental accomplishments.

19. What were the qualities of soul that explain Carey's greatness?

20. Copy several of Carey's memorable sayings. Mark the occasion and significance of each.

21. What impressed you most, relative to Carey's death?

22. Note the problems Carey had to face.

23. Note these challenging statistics.

> The population of the world at the time of this writing is about 5.3 billion. Carey estimated the world's population to be 731 million, of whom seven–ninths were Pagans or Mohammedans. Approximately how many more unsaved souls are there in the world today than in Carey's day? Consider the staggering import of these facts.
>
> The population of India is increasing at the rate of about 15.4 million each year. Only a small percentage are being reached for Christ. According to best estimates, the population of India when Carey arrived in 1793 was approximately 200 million. According to latest figures and estimates at the time of this writing, today's population is in excess of 684

million. In other words, there are over three times as many unsaved souls in India today as when Carey first arrived. What a need! What a challenge!

24. For additional data on religious beliefs and practices of India:

E.W. Hopkins—*Religions of India*
J.N.D. Anderson—*The World's Religions*, chap. IV & V
Ione Lowman—*Non-Christian Religions*, chapter IV

GEORGE GRENFELL

A Light in Congo Darkness
(1849 – 1906)

Huge crocodiles dozing on the muddy banks of the mighty Congo sullenly opened their beady eyes to gaze at the strange monster, then hastily plunged into the river. The cause of their alarm was the small steamer, *The Peace*, the first ship ever to breast the Congo waters under steam power. The crocodiles were not alone in being alarmed at the sight and sound of the throbbing steamer. Frequently the Africans were so startled they fled pell-mell into the jungles or were so aroused they swarmed out in their canoes to do battle.

Coming in sight of a large village, the white captain shouted orders to his black crew. The boat slowed up and drew within fifty yards of the shore. The captain's keen eyes observed that the people were friendly, so he climbed down into the ship's canoe and was paddled ashore by several of his men. Scores of natives crowded around to look at the strange man with the white face, who proceeded to tell them that he was a missionary who had come to bring the light and love of God.

"Do you mean to suggest that we are living in darkness?" asked the chief somewhat petulantly.

Just then the missionary heard the sound of sobbing. Making his way through the crowd, he found two little girls bound with cords and tied to a tree. "What does this mean?" he asked.

With no evidence of shame, the chief told how he and his warriors armed with spears and bows and arrows had gone far up the river in their canoes on a raiding expedition against another tribe. "And these girls," continued the chief, "are part of the booty we captured. They are my slaves and are tied here until somebody buys them."

Touched by the sight of the trembling, sobbing girls, the white man promptly handed over some beads and cloth, took the girls down to the river and into the canoe. They kept wondering as they were paddled out to the *S.S. Peace*, if the white man would be cruel to them.

The ship started upstream again and the astonished girls knew no bounds as they sped swiftly past banks of forests and villages. On and on they went for several hours. Eventually, the *Peace* turned a bend in the river and the missionary saw a whole fleet of canoes filled with fierce looking warriors, some holding spears, others with bows in their hands and poisoned arrows drawn to the head.

These Congo men were enraged because, just a few days earlier, people from down-river had suddenly raided their town, burned many of their huts, killed many of the villagers and taken away some of their children. They conjectured since the *Peace* had also come from down-river, those on board must likewise be enemies.

At a signal from the chief, the tribe's fierce battle cry was sounded and a shower of spears and arrows struck the steamer. One of them nearly pierced the missionary captain. Suddenly one of the little slave girls began to shout and wave her hand. "What is it?" asked the missionary.

"See!" she answered excitedly, pointing to a warrior standing up in a canoe and preparing to hurl a spear. "That is my brother and this is my town!"

"Call to him and attract his attention!" said the captain. The little girl shouted as loudly as she could, but the African warriors were making a fearful din, and the only answer was a hail of spears and arrows. Hastily, the captain issued an order to the steamer's African engineer, and in a moment a wild, piercing shriek rent the air, then several others in quick succession. The warriors ceased their yelling and stood as if turned to stone. Never before had they heard the whistle of a steamer!

"Shout again—quickly!" said the captain to the little Congo girl.

Instantly the shrill, childish voice rang out across the water, calling first her brother's name and then her own. The astonished warrior dropped his spear, seized his oar and quickly paddled to the steamer. In response to the captain's instructions, the girl told how the white man in "the big canoe that smokes" had found her and the other girl in the town of their enemies, had saved them from slavery, had brought them safely home, and now was going to set them free.

The story passed quickly from one canoe to another as the two girls were taken ashore; and as the captain walked up the village street, all the warriors who had tried to kill him only a few minutes before, were now gazing wonderingly at the white friend who had brought back the daughters they thought they had lost forever. Now they were ready to listen to his story of the great Father God who sent His Son to be the Light of this dark and sinful world.

This remarkable ship captain was George Grenfell, pioneer missionary in the vast Congo region of Africa. The statement of Jesus concerning John the Baptist, "He was a burning and shining light," was almost constantly in his mind. He was convinced that the desperate need of the whole wide world is the saving light of the Gospel of Christ and that it was his business to take that light to Congo's millions. His life may be summarized in three statements:

a light begins to shine, a shining light lightens Congo's darkness, and a burning light burns out.

I. A LIGHT BEGINS TO SHINE

George Grenfell was born the son of a carpenter August 21, 1849 in Sancreed, near Land's End in Cornwall, England. When he was three years old, the family moved to Birmingham where George and his brother began to attend the Sunday school of the Heneage Street Baptist Church. At fifteen, in the spiritual aftermath of the great revival of 1859, he was soundly converted and baptized. Thus the candle of his life was lit by contact with Him who is "this dark world's light," and very soon thereafter began to think seriously of being a light-bearer for Christ in the Dark Continent. Like *Mackay of Uganda*, *Laws of Livingstonia*, and others, Grenfell found in David Livingstone his hero and human inspiration. The Pathfinder's books were eagerly devoured as fast as they came from the press.

About the time of his baptism, George left school and became an apprentice in a large hardware and machinery plant. Here he acquired that knowledge of machinery which proved to be inestimable in value during his subsequent missionary career. Too, it was while in this plant that he lost the sight of one eye.

George aligned himself with a group of zealous young men connected with the Heneage Street Church. Their Sunday, beginning with a morning prayer meeting at seven, usually included seven services with tract distribution and personal work during the intervals. Then, after such a strenuous Sunday, they regularly attended a Monday morning Greek Bible Study at the minister's house at 6:30. Moreover, they published a paper called *Mission Work*, the object of which was to set before its readers "proofs from all quarters of the globe that the Gospel is, as of old, the power of God unto salvation." Its editor was George Grenfell.

This sort of consecrated enthusiasm of Christ was needed in Africa. Finally, convinced of a divine call to be a missionary, George gave up business at the age of twenty-four and entered the Baptist College at Bristol. After a year's training he was accepted by the Baptist Missionary Society for service in Africa and sailed with the veteran, Alfred Saker who was in England on furlough. They reached the Cameroons in January, 1875. Early the next year Grenfell married Miss Mary Hakes who died in less than a year. Grenfell experienced his first great sorrow.

Six hundred miles south of the Cameroons, the Congo, the world's second largest river, enters the Atlantic. A Hundred miles from the sea, navigation was barred by a series of cataracts beyond which the map was blank. How incredible that this great river, the Congo (or the Lualaba), should have flowed almost entirely across the African continent for thousands of years and yet, until seventy-five years ago, its vast basin, an area as large as all of Europe, was a land of mystery. On one occasion a native, who was said to have travelled rather extensively, was questioned by a European traveler.

"Do you know where this river goes?"

"It flows north and east."

"And then?"

"It keeps on flowing north and east."

"And then?"

"Allah yallim—God knows."

Until seventy-five years ago, that was the sum of human knowledge on the subject—"Allah yallim." Livingstone, to be sure, had reached the Lualaba in 1871 at Nyangwe. There he wrote his burning indictment of the slave trade. At first he thought he had found the long-sought source of the Nile but later suspected it might turn out to be the Congo. He urged the powerful Mohammedan, Tiptu Tib, to help secure him supplies and carriers for the purpose of ascending the river. The appeal fell on deaf ears, and Livingstone had to content himself with exploring the upper reaches of the Lualaba and its eastern branch, the Luapula, until 1873 when at Chitambo's village he knelt down to die, his work for Christ and Africa bravely done. As for the further course of the Lualaba—for more than 2,000 miles—"Allah yallim."

After their heroic odyssey of 999 days in crossing Africa, Henry M. Stanley and his sadly depleted, half-starved caravan reached Boma, near the mouth of the Congo on August 8, 1877. But some months before Stanley's sensational achievement had turned the world's eyes on Equatorial Africa, two men were independently planning to plant a chain of mission stations far in the interior or even across the continent. One was Grenfell, then laboring in the Cameroons. The other was Robert Arthington who, in England, had dedicated his fortune to Christ and himself to poverty in order to supply money to various missionary societies. This noble man deprived himself of all but the barest of necessities, wore the same coat for seventeen years, and even begrudged the use of candles, that he might devote the utmost farthing to world evangelization.

On May 14, 1877, Arthington offered the Baptist Society 1,000 pounds for the purpose of taking "the blessed light of the Gospel" to the Congo region. With astounding vision he wrote: "I hope we shall soon have a steamer on the Congo, to carry the Gospel eastward, and south and north of the river, as the way may open, as far as Nyangwe." The Society did not act, however, until the publication of Stanley's letter in the *Daily Telegraph*, September 17, 1877.

Early in 1878 Grenfell was on his way along the bank of the Congo. "So," as stated by C. H. Patton in the *Lure of Africa*, "the Baptists were the first to see and to seize the great opening made by Stanley's explorations." Grenfell encountered almost insuperable difficulties. But finally, after thirteen attempts, after splashing through swamps and tramping through grass fifteen feet high, and after frequent, perilous escapes from savages after one of his companions had been severely wounded, passed the cataracts and reached Stanley Pool in February, 1881. By means of the vast system of waterways created by the Congo and its numerous tributaries, some twenty-five million people were at reach. Canoes were available, but they were slow and dangerous. Hippopotami often upset them, after which crocodiles feasted upon the occupants. The solution to the problem was a steamer, as had been suggested several years earlier by Robert Arthington, who now provided one thousand pounds toward its construction and three thousand pounds toward its perpetual maintenance. "I believe the time is come," wrote this noble hearted man, "when we should place a steamer on the Congo River, where we can sail uninterruptedly north-eastward into the heart of Africa for many hundreds of miles and bring the glad tidings of the everlasting Gospel to thousands of human beings who now are ignorant of the way of life and of immortality."

Grenfell, who had remarried in 1879, left his wife on the Congo and proceeded to England where he supervised the construction of the *Peace*, a screw steamer 78 feet in length drawing twelve inches of water. After it had been tested on the Thames, it was taken apart, put in 800 packages weighing 65 pounds each and shipped to the mouth of the Congo. A thousand men carried the vessel and necessary food supplies up the river and past the rapids to Stanley Pool. Grenfell had brought with him a young missionary engineer whose special assignment was to put the vessel together and then keep it in good running order. Soon after reaching African soil, he fell sick and died. Two other engineers were promptly sent out from England, but both died within a few weeks.

So Grenfell himself had to undertake the gigantic task of putting the ship together, a task he successfully accomplished. He declared that the *Peace* was "prayed together." Certainly much prayer, as well as hard work and ingenuity, had been necessary. Finally the vessel was launched. Steam was up and the *Peace* began to move. "She lives, Master! She lives!" shouted the excited Africans.

At last George Grenfell was able to begin, in earnest, his remarkable work of missionary exploration and of establishing mission stations as centers of light. He thought of himself as a successor of John the Baptist, of whom John the Apostle wrote: "The same came to bear witness of the Light, that all men through Him might believe." And it was Grenfell's great yearning to be worthy of the tribute Jesus paid the Forerunner, "He was a burning and a shining light."

"I am the light of the world." A life cannot shine until lit at that resplendent Flame!

"Let your light so shine." A life is lighted to lighten! "He was a *shining* light."

II. A SHINING LIGHT LIGHTENS THE CONGO DARKNESS

The maiden voyage of the *Peace* covered twelve hundred miles and brought many memorable adventures. Captain Grenfell went half way to Stanley Falls and turned aside to explore several of the chief tributaries. Having decided on Lukolela as the site of a mission station, he stayed there two days making friends with the people. As he stopped in the villages, his heart was saddened to encounter ever fresh examples of the hideousness and depravity of barbarism. In certain areas, he found many evidences of fetishism, with its many facets and its degrading idolatry. "It was," he said, "a wondrous joy to take for the first time, the light of life into those regions of darkness, cruelty, and death."

In order to indicate something of the abysmal darkness into which Grenfell brought "the light of life" and to show the unrealism of those who oppose missions on the grounds that the heathen should not be disturbed in the tranquility and beauty of their native religious customs, a few facts and incidents will be cited.

Grenfell found six general types of atrocious practices being committed by Congo peoples, all of which were either definitely a part of their religious system or an expression of the depravity from which their religion was powerless to lift them. These types were: burial murders, witchcraft cruelties, slave raiding, cannibalism, sensuality, and sadistic methods of punishment.

Burial Murders

Among practically all the tribes of the Congo area, no free person of any consequence could be buried without the sacrifice of one or more lives. This was due to their belief that the dead nobility must not be ushered into the spirit world alone. There must be at least one wife, one servant or, in the case of a chief, king, or queen, many servants to accompany the deceased and to carry on the spirit life as nearly as possible along the lines of the terrestrial existence. The practice of interring pottery, cloth, beads, cooking utensils and various implements involved a staggering waste of property, but much more tragic was the waste of human life.

In his diary dated July 7, 1889, Grenfell relates:

> We hear two people are tied up at Mungula's, ready to be buried alive. The man killed yesterday was decapitated; his skull will soon adorn Mungula's house. The woman killed yesterday was beaten to death with sticks. At 3:15 I went and started to protest against burying the two victims with the corpse. The wild looking executioner untied the young woman and took her into the house where the grave had been dug. I followed him and found the young man who was to be her fellow victim

already seated by the side of the grave...I rebuked the old chief sharply and explained to the onlookers that God, who had given life, would call to account those who took it away. My heart was very hot within me to see the tears of the poor crying victims of such cruel customs. Three times I warned Mungula plainly that he would have to meet me and these innocent victims before God's throne and answer for their lives. But we had not turned our backs more than a few seconds when the poor victims were thrown into the grave and the corpse placed on their bodies. They were speedily covered in and buried alive.

Again he writes: "April 13, 1890. We hear that on Manga being dead three people were killed yesterday and that four more are tied up for today."

Upon returning home from a trip, Grenfell states:

June 17, 1890. While I was away, Ngoie brought a slave to sell. James, my native helper, would not buy. In less than five minutes the slave's head was off and lying on the beach. One of Boyambula's men has lost his wife just recently and has killed nine slaves.

On April 15, 1889, Grenfell writes:

James tells me that some eight people have been killed to accompany chief Ibaka. His wives had a woman given them to kill. They dispatched her with their hoes, as their custom is. Two or three were buried alive, others beaten to death with sticks, and one or two drowned.

Here is an extract from his Diary dated January 14, 1889: "I learn on reaching Lukolela that when Mangaba and another chief died recently some dozen people were killed—Mangaba's principal wife for one and a little child for a pillow!"

The activities connected with the death of a great Baluba chief are thus described by a missionary:

> *When an important chief expires, a young slave is slain and laid by the corpse for two days. After two or three days of ceaseless lamentation another slave is sacrificed. When the funeral procession is set in motion two men are beaten to death with clubs and thrown across the public road without burial; it is their mission to tell passers by that their master has gone along that way to his last dwelling. When the grave has been dug two female slaves of the dead man descend therein and lie beside the corpse. If the wretched women do not willingly submit to this ordeal, they are bound and compelled to do so. After six slaves have been butchered and thrown into the tomb, the place is filled with dirt, the two female slaves thus being buried alive.*

Witchcraft Cruelties

Relatively speaking, burial customs slew thousands while witchcraft ordeals slew tens of thousands. By virtue of these ordeals, the population in one single area was reduced from about ten thousand in 1845 to two thousand in 1885. In all Central Africa it was well-nigh impossible, in native belief, to die a natural death. Illness and death were normally caused by the use of occult powers or "the evil eye." If a man or woman was killed by a crocodile, leopard, buffalo, elephant or python, the animal in question was believed to be a witch in disguise or at least under the direction of a witch. All sickness, except in extreme old age, was attributed to witchcraft. Consequently, after every death from either disease or accident, a witch doctor was called in to "smell out" the guilty party, who was forthwith made to undergo the poison ordeal. If he was lucky enough to vomit the poison, he was innocent, but if he died, which usually happened, he was clearly guilty. In frequent instances public opinion was so excited, the accused person was killed at sight whereupon his body was cut open and searched for the conclusive proof of witchcraft, namely, the presence of a gallbladder. Since every normal human being has a gallbladder, all accused and slaughtered persons were proven to be witches.

A missionary, describing a poison ordeal, says that the witch doctor or the medicine man usually came forth with an animal skin around his loins, his body painted with ochre and carrying a spear, an axe and an executioner's knife. He proceeded to prepare a large dose of poison, made from the bark of a certain tree which the accused person usually drank readily, expecting to be vindicated, knowing that he had not used witchcraft powers. If he threw up the poison, he was innocent; and the person who accused him was likely to be caught and cut to pieces by the prisoner's relatives. But if he could not bring up the poison quickly, and this was usually the case, he sank to the ground in terrific pain. This was clear proof of his guilt and the relatives of the person whom his sorceries were supposed to have killed, hurled themselves upon him and cut him to pieces.

In his translation, Grenfell learned that there was no word for "forgiveness." Unhappy Congo: where no one knew what it was to forgive or be forgiven!

Slave Raiding

As indicated in the story of the two slave girls rescued by Grenfell, raiding for the purpose of securing slaves was a very common, as well as a devastating, practice. Such raids were undertaken to replenish the slave labor supply, which was constantly being depleted by burial murders, poison ordeals, harsh treatment or disease.

Slaves were also sought because of their market value, especially where Arab or Portuguese slave traders could be contacted. This form of "man's inhumanity to man" brought indescribable suffering.

Cannibalism

A further reason for the slave raids mentioned above was to secure victims for cannibal feasts. When Grenfell reached the principal Bangala settlement in November, 1888, the people were busy killing and cutting up slaves in preparation for a feast. The pathway into the town was lined by hideous rows of skulls, and most of the people were decorated with necklaces of human teeth taken from captives they had eaten.

Being thin sometimes had special advantages in the Congo. As Grenfell went about in the steamer, he often took s c h o o l b o y s with him to sing the Gospel and perhaps act as interpreters. On numerous occasions he was entreated to sell a fat boatman in his employ or some of the schoolboys who, coming from the shores of the salt sea, were considered especially appetizing. One day a lad rushed up to him and said: "Master, three of us were captured. They ate the other two, but I was so thin they turned me loose!"

In most sections of the Congo, man was the most voracious of all the carnivore. When the son of chief Mata Bwiki was asked if he had eaten human flesh he replied: "Ah yes! And I wish I could eat everybody on earth."

On the Mubangi River there was a much greater demand for human flesh than the local markets could supply. The people on the Lulongo chiefly made their living by conducting raids and selling the captives to the Mubangi. In *Pioneering on the Congo*, a missionary says:

> *They fought the unsuspecting and unprepared people, killed many in the process and brought the rest home with them. They divided up their human booty and kept them in their towns, tied up and kept alive with a minimum of food. A party would be made up and sold*

*to the Mubangi for ivory. The purchasers would then
feed up their starvelings until they were fat enough for
the market, then butcher and sell them in pieces.*

One of the Bangala chiefs visited by Missionary Bentley in 1887 had already eaten seven of his wives. He was careful to explain, however, that he had not done this selfishly, because he had bidden the relatives to each feast in turn, thus avoiding family unpleasantness!

Among the Manbettu and Mabode tribes, the bodies of enemies slain in battle were either eaten at once or carried off in long slices as provisions for subsequent use. The prisoners were taken along and penned up like cattle for future consumption. According to Torday:

> *It often happens among the Ngombe tribes that the
> poor creature destined for the knife is exposed for sale
> in the market. He walks to and fro and epicures come
> to examine the leg, breast, or head. The portions which
> are purchased are marked off with lines of colored ochre.
> When the entire body is sold, the wretch is slain.*

The first place in this Chapter of Horrors must be given to the Nsakara, the Nyamnyam, the Basoka and the Manyema. The Nsakara specialized in eating the victims sacrificed on the graves of chiefs, consuming these holocausts of slaughtered slaves in elaborate feasts lasting several days. The carnivorous lust of the Nyamnyam and Basoka led them to eat dead bodies, unless death was due to an infectious disease. The Manyema were human vultures who deliberately ate dead bodies several days old without cooking them.

Sensuality

Many other types of barbaric degeneracy could be cited. Grenfell says: "The chief characteristics of Balobo people are drunkenness, immorality and cruelty, from each of which vices spring actions almost too terrible to describe." In one place of which he speaks, the death of a chief's wife was followed by four days of "unbridled license in every species of sensuality," in addition to the sacrifice of four slaves.

Methods of Punishment

Methods of punishment were in part prompted by a sadistic enjoyment in inflicting pain. "Thieves," says Grenfell, "are often punished by gagging with a stick thrust through the flesh of the cheeks. Sometimes they are tormented by having their bodies rubbed with pepper before being decapitated." Guilt for petty offenses was often determined by having the accused thrust his arm into a pot of boiling water. If his arm was unscalded, he was innocent. Among the Ngombe, women often times were required to put a stringent sap under one eyelid. If innocent, the eye would remain undamaged. This ordeal resulted in a large number of one-eyed women in this region.

When a well-known chief, Maidi, was too old to conduct expeditions against other tribes, he set about tormenting his own subjects who failed to please his fancy. He would shut up women in pens with famished dogs. Poor wretches tied to trees were left to starve while other victims were buried up to their necks and left alive for wild beasts.

For almost twenty-five years Grenfell steamed along the Congo and its tributaries in either the *Peace* or its larger successors, the *Goodwill* or the *Endeavor*, establishing mission stations and taking the light of redemption's story to those dwelling in dark habitats. In one letter he says:

> *I cannot write you a tithe of the woes that have come unto my notice and have made my heart bleed as I have voyaged along. Cruelty, sin and slavery are as millstones*

around the necks of the people, dragging them down into a sea of sorrows. I pray that God will speedily make manifest to these poor brethren of ours that light which is the light of life, even Jesus Christ, our living Lord.

The light! The light of life!

It was that light he sought to diffuse!

In the habitations of darkness, "He was a SHINING light."

III. A BURNING LIGHT BURNS OUT

To be "a burning and shining light" was Grenfell's passionate desire. Like John the Baptist, he was a shining light because he was first and always a burning light. Taking the "blessed Gospel light" to Congo's wretched millions called forth his utmost energy, and in this service his flame never flickered, despite manifold sorrows.

There were the sorrows of pity. At Stanley Falls he saw the notorious Tippu Tib, the wholesale slave raider of Central and Eastern Africa. The devastations and crimes of the Arabs made him sick at heart. "We counted," he says, "twenty burned villages and thousands of fugitive canoes." Among the smoking ruins of one of these villages, a man called out, "We have nothing left, nothing! Our houses are burned, our plantations are destroyed, and our women and children have been taken away into slavery."

There were sorrows of anxiety. Grenfell's life was in peril countless times, and he admitted that it was difficult to keep one's spirits up with disaster in constant threat. He writes at the end of one of his voyages:

> *Thank God we are safely back. It might have been otherwise, for we have encountered perils not a few. But*

the winds which were sometimes simply terrific, and the rocks, which knocked three holes in the steamer when we were fleeing from cannibals, have not wrecked us. We have been attacked by natives about twenty different times; we have been stoned and shot at with arrows, and have been the mark for spears more than we can count.

There were the sorrows of indignation. Grenfell was sadly disillusioned by the administration of the Congo Free State by the Belgians. Aware of the chaos and savagery associated with native rule, he expected a great improvement from the rule of the Belgians and assisted them in many ways, notably by serving as a capitol commissioner to settle the state's southern boundary in 1891. Even prior to this, however, he began to have serious misgivings as he saw the Belgian octopus, King Leopold, fastening itself on the Congo by enunciating a monstrous doctrine stating this region and its inhabitants were his personal property. His disillusionment corresponded to that of the Africans, who at first, were charmed to discover the value of raw rubber, and how it would enable them to buy the glittering trinkets and cloth they desired.

Before long, however, with spirits crushed by forced labor, floggings, imprisonments, mutilations and murders, the Africans cried out in bitter despair, "Rubber is death!" When, therefore, in 1890 the Belgian authorities commandeered the *Peace* to further their own schemes, Grenfell made such an effective protest in England that the steamer was restored, and the Belgian King bestowed on him, at a personal interview in Brussels, the insignia: "Chevalier of the Order of Leopold." Somewhat humorously, Grenfell described himself as feeling "like a barn door with a brass knocker." It was a poignant sorrow to learn how he had spent his last years observing King Leopold hypocritically professing and bestowing thousands in philanthropic efforts for the uplift of Central Africa. He was, in reality, sending his myrmidons over the Congo with orders demanding the people to produce more rubber while filling his personal coffers with millions saturated with African blood. The Belgians also hindered him in his efforts to establish mission stations all the way across Central Africa. By patient persistence, he succeeded in establishing stations farther and farther along the Congo, some as far as Yakusu and Yalemba.

Grenfell was indignant at the preferential treatment accorded to the Catholics and that the Catholics, instead of seeking the untouched masses of heathenism, made a special point to establish a rival mission wherever he established a station and sought by various devices to subvert his converts.

Added to the other sorrows were the sorrows of death. Africa was already known as the White Man's Grave. The toll of missionary life was greatest in the Congo, which was called "the shortcut to heaven." In 1883-84, seven of Grenfell's colleagues finished their course after only a few months of service. In 1885, four men died in three months, and in 1887, six missionaries fell in five months. In other years there were distressing losses. Some people at the home base felt the loss in life was too enormous and the Congo Mission should be abandoned or at least curtailed. But Grenfell was of a different spirit. In 1888, he wrote to the Society: "We can't continue as we are. It is either advance or retreat. But if it is retreat, you must not count on me. I will be no party to it, and you will have to do without me."

The sorrows of death came even closer and almost crushed him. He had buried his first wife in the Cameroons; and it was his sad lot to bury four of his children on the Congo. These graves were as milestones along the river as he pushed farther and farther inland. His grave was destined to be the farthest of all.

Grenfell's last years were darkened by the sorrows of illness but gladdened by the sweet joys of harvest. In 1902, he writes of the work at Bolobo: "Our services are crowded as they have never been before. God's Spirit is manifestly working." In his voyages up and down the river, he saw many evidences of happy change. Poison ordeals, burial murders and other abhorrent practices were diminishing, and "the light of life" was beginning to dawn in many dark hearts. Concerning one place he states:

> *Just twenty years have elapsed since I first landed at the foot of this cliff and was driven off at the point of native spears. The reception this time was very different. The teacher and a little crowd of school children stood on the beach to welcome us.*

In 1905 he says of another place:

> *It was here that, twenty-one years ago, we first came into view of the burning villages of the big Arab slave raid of 1884. This time, as we were looking for a good camping place, we suddenly heard strike up 'All Hail the Power' from on board one of the big fishing canoes hidden among the reeds so that we had not observed it. What a glorious welcome! Whose heart would not be moved to hear 'Crown Him Lord of All' under such circumstances? I little thought to live to see so blessed a change and my heart went forth in praise.*

He believed that love, which is the essence of Christianity, should and would find expression in disinterested service. He established a printing press, taught brick making, treated the sick, engaged in translation, and rendered such distinguished service in exploration and cartography that the Royal Geographical Society awarded him a Gold Medal in 1886. He was the first person to steam up the Congo, exploring many of its tributaries.

In a letter to a friend, he wrote:

I know John 3:16, and that's good enough holding ground for my anchor...Our Christianity is too much a matter of words and far too little a matter of works. One might think works were of the Devil by the assiduity with which the great proportion of church members keep clear of them.

Soon after opening up a new station at Yalemba, near Stanley Falls, he fell ill with haematuric fever. His native boys, who affectionately called him Tata or Father, gently took him on board the *Peace* and steamed down to Bapoto. He rapidly grew weaker, and his soul departed July 1, 1901. His last words were, "Jesus is mine."

One of the native boys, Balsuti, concludes the account of the burial with these beautiful words: "Then we sang another hymn. Last of all we closed the grave. And so the death of Tata finished." In the words of Hawker, "Well written, O Balsuti: 'The death of Tata finished,' but not the life!"

When Jesus referred to John the Baptist as "a burning and shining light," He was thinking of a candle, which must pay a heavy price to shine. What does it cost a candle to furnish light? It costs its very existence! It costs everything! Even so, to take the light of the saving Gospel into the dark Congo cost Grenfell and the early missionaries everything. Who else will pay that price?

GEORGE GRENFELL

QUESTIONS, TOPICS, AND ASSIGNMENTS
FOR STUDY

1. In what areas of the Dark Continent did Grenfell work for Christ?

2. What was the chief means of travel among the villagers there?

3. What was the relationship between villages? Were neighboring tribes inclined to be friendly or hostile?

4. How much had modern civilization influenced the life in this country when Grenfell started his work for the Lord?

5. Did these people approve of slavery? How do you know?

6. Did Grenfell's family background and his childhood experiences make it harder for him to launch out for the Lord? Why or why not?

7. From what physical handicap did he suffer?

8. In what phases of the work in the Heneage Street Baptist Church in Birmingham, England, did Grenfell participate?

9. How old was he when he sailed for the foreign field?

10. How much was known about the Congo River in 1875? How did this limit the work for Christ's Kingdom?

11. What great Christian explorer was also laboring in Africa at this time? What great event concerning this man took place during Grenfell's first years there?

12. What were the problems involved in traveling?

13. Who supervised the construction of the steamboat *Peace*? Who paid for it? Why?

14. Name the six general types of atrocities given in the chapter. Summarize the probable sense of values these people had using the following as clues:

    A.   Value placed on a human life
    B.   Emphasis or lack of emphasis on burial
    C.   Attitude toward torture

15. How many lives were sacrificed at the death of an important Baluba chief? What does this show about part A in question 14 listed above?

16. Define witchcraft. Decide whether you think it was believed to be evil or good.

17. Describe the poison ordeal.

18. What word had no Congo translation? What significance does this have for us as Christians?

19. Give two reasons for slave raids?

20. Review the chapter and find the ten cannibalistic tribes mentioned. Look up at least one in a World Encyclopedia to find five important facts about the tribe's characteristics or consult Henry M. Stanley's *Through the Dark Continent* (Harper, New York, 1878).

21. What types of sorrows did Grenfell experience?

22. What relationship did Grenfell have with King Leopold?

23. Why was the Congo work almost stopped entirely?

24. What difference did Grenfell see in the receptiveness of the people after twenty years of laboring?

25. What were the chief phases of his ministry?

26. Summarize Grenfell's life by giving a comparison of it with a candle. You need not follow the material pertaining to it in this chapter.

27. One of the most common aspects of primitive religion is fetishism; it proliferates over wide areas such as Africa. For further study, consult the following:

E. D. Soper—*Religions of Mankind*, pp. 58-61

F. B. Jevons—*Introduction to the Study of Comparative Religion*, pp. 105-107.

J. G. Frazer—*The Golden Bough*, Vol. 1.

ADONIRAM JUDSON

THE APOSTLE OF THE LOVE OF CHRIST IN BURMA
(1788 – 1850)

There it was—the site of the historic Let-ma-yoon prison, famous for its heathen horrors and its Christian conquests. Soon after commencing my missionary service in Burma, I went to Mandalay, then through the dense jungle growth to the memorial slab marking the site where Adoniram and Ann Judson, America's first Missionaries, endured such incredible sufferings as ambassadors of Christ.

As I stood there, I recalled the confident prediction Judson made in 1816, in his first tract for the Burmese people: "About one hundred or at most, two hundred years hence the religion of Buddha, of Brahma, of Mohammed and of Rome, with all other false religions, will disappear and the religion of Christ will pervade the whole world." Why is it, as we hasten toward the termination of the two hundred years of which Judson spoke, that the unsaved multitudes of earth are greater by at least one thousand million than they were when Judson made his prediction?

In a day when the cause of world evangelism is so sadly languishing, it will be a humbling and inspiring experience for the American Christians to turn aside and expose their souls afresh to the story of one magnificently captivated by the love of Christ. The love of Christ was his hope, his incentive, and his consolation. The love of Christ sang and sobbed and shouted its way through all the changing scenes, manifold trials and monumental accomplishments of the five great epochs of his life.

I. THE LOVE OF CHRIST CLEANSED HIS POLLUTED HEART

In the Baptist meeting house in Malden, Massachusetts, the traveler will find a marble tablet bearing the following:

IN MEMORIAM

REV. ADONIRAM JUDSON
BORN AUG. 9, 1788
DIED APRIL 12, 1850
MALDEN, HIS BIRTHPLACE
THE OCEAN, HIS SEPULCHRE
CONVERTED BURMANS AND
THE BURMAN BIBLE,
HIS MONUMENT
HIS RECORD IS ON HIGH

Judson was a very precocious boy. When only three years of age he learned to read under the tutelage of his mother while his father was absent on a journey. The father's astonishment was great upon returning to hear his young son read to him a chapter from the Bible.

He grew up in a devout Christian home. His father, a Congregational minister, cherished the fond hope that his son would follow in his footsteps. But Adoniram was enamored of his brilliance and could not think of wasting his superb talents in so dull a calling as the ministry. Having vanquished all rivals in intellectual contests, he graduated at nineteen from Providence College (now Brown University) as valedictorian. He entertained the most extravagant ambitions and his imagination ran wild as he contemplated his future eminence. He pictured himself as an orator, greater than

Demosthenes, swaying the multitudes with his eloquence; as a second Homer, writing immortal poems; as a second Alexander the Great, weeping because there were no more worlds to conquer.

Judson was not only inordinately ambitious; he was also openly atheistic. It was during the early nineteenth century while Judson was in college that French infidelity swept over the country. With only three or four exceptions, all the students of Yale were avowed infidels and preferred to call each other by the names of leading infidels such as Tom Paine or Voltaire, instead of their own names.

Providence College did not escape the contaminations of this vile flood of skepticism. In the class just above that of Judson was a young, outspoken atheist by the name of Ernest, who was exceptionally gifted, witty and clever. An intimate friendship developed between these two brilliant young men, with the result that, to the extreme mortification of his father and mother, Judson also became a bold exponent of infidelity. When his father sought to argue with him, he quickly demonstrated his intellectual superiority, but he had no answer to his mother's tears and solemn warnings.

One day he set out on horseback on an adventurous tour through several states. He joined a band of strolling players and lived, as he himself related later, "a wild, reckless life." Leaving the troupe after a few weeks, he continued his trip on horseback, stipping on a certain historic night at a country inn. Apologetically, the landlord explained that, only one room being vacant, he would be obliged to put him next door to a young man who was extremely ill—probably dying.

"I'll take the room," said Judson. "Death has no terrors for me. You see, I'm an atheist."

Judson retired but sleep eluded him. The partition was very thin and for long hours he listened to the groans of the dying man—groans of agony and groans of despair. "The poor fellow is evidently dying in terror. I suppose I should go to his assistance, but what could I say that would help him?" thought Judson to himself; and he shivered at the very thought of going into the presence of the dying man. He felt a blush of shame steal over him. What would his late unbelieving companions think if they knew of his weakness? Above all, what would witty, brilliant Ernest say, if he knew? As he tried to compose himself, the dreadful cries from the next room continued. He pulled the blankets over his head but still he heard the awful sounds—and shuddered! Finally, all became quiet. At dawn, having had no sleep, he rose and inquired of the innkeeper concerning his fellow lodger.

"He is dead!" "Dead!" replied Judson. "And do you know who he was?"

"Yes," the innkeeper answered, "he was a graduate of Providence College, a young fellow named Ernest."

Judson was overwhelmed by the news that the young man who died the previous night in the adjoining room in evident terror of death was his college friend Ernest, who had led him into infidelity. For many hours the words "Dead! Lost! Lost!" kept ringing in his ears. There was now just one place that beckoned him. Turning his horse's direction, he went home and begged his father and mother to help him find a faith that would stand the test of life and of death, of time and eternity.

The brilliant young skeptic realized at last that he needed:

A faith for the testing of life!

A faith for the exigencies of death!

A faith for time and eternity!

At this time of acute spiritual struggle, when his mind was filled with the dark clouds of infidelity and his soul enveloped with the black darkness of sin, he turned to the Word of God. Before long his heart was cleansed, his mind illumined and his soul enraptured by the incoming tide of the love of Christ. Henceforth Ephesians 3:17-19 was his great text, and the love of Christ was his theme. Henceforth he was magnificently captivated by the love of Christ as he explored the mystic meaning and the abounding fullness of its fourfold dimension—its breath and length, its depth and height.

II. THE LOVE OF CHRIST SANCTIFIED HIS AMBITIONS

As a student at Andover Seminary, Judson heard and read of the work that William Carey and his associates were opening up in India. This influenced him to give serious consideration to the question of foreign missions. His first conclusion was that surely the love of Christ, which had so marvelously banished the darkness from his own soul, was meant for all mankind. By day he was haunted by the vision of vast nations bound and dying in the darksome prison house of sin. By night he spent long, sleepless hours contemplating the hapless condition of teeming multitudes beyond the sea sinking into Christless graves. But it was not easy to find and accept his place in the divine program. There was a terrific struggle in his soul between his worldly ambitions and the claims of the love of Christ. Then one epochal day he went out into the woods and fell down, praying: "More than all else, I long to please Thee, my Lord. What wilt Thou have me to do?" As he prayed, he felt the presence of Jesus close beside him and heard His voice saying, "Go to the uttermost parts and preach the Gospel of My love. I send you forth, like Paul, as a witness to distant nations." Judson, like Paul, rose up determined not to be disobedient to his Lord's commission.

He soon gathered a group of kindred spirits. Among these were four young men who had come to Andover from William's College: Samuel J. Mills, Jr., James Richards, Luther Rice and Gordon

Hall. Already, while in college, these young men had taken refuge from a storm under a haystack and had solemnly dedicated their lives to take the Gospel to the "far away places." But there was no missionary society to send them forth. The question which now burdened Judson and his associates was that which Paul raised, "How shall we preach unless we be sent?" In response to the challenge of these consecrated young lives, a missionary society was formed, consecrated money poured in, the necessary equipment was provided and the missionaries arranged to depart. On the 5th day of February, 1812, Judson was married to Ann Hasseltine, who was destined to become the heroic "Ann of Ava." The next day he and his fellow appointees received solemn ordination at Salem and on the 19th, embarked on the sailship *Caravan* bound for Calcutta.

During the long voyage the Judsons changed not only their physical, but also their denominational, latitude and longitude. As the result of a protracted study of the New Testament in the original Greek, they decided to become Baptists. Upon reaching Calcutta they had blessed fellowship with the English Baptist missionaries, Carey, Marshman and Ward, and formally aligned themselves with the Baptists.

This was a serious decision. They could no longer expect support from the churches that sent them out. Would the Baptists of the United States, at that time a very feeble people, rise up to their support? Just at this critical juncture another difficulty arose. They were peremptorily ordered out of India by the East India Company on the expectation that the missionaries would interfere with its nefarious trading practices. After a long journey to the Isle of France, they returned to India and landed at Madras. Again, the East India Company ordered them to leave the country immediately else they would be deported back to England and America. Accordingly, they embarked on the *Georgianna*, which Judson described as a "crazy old vessel." For three weeks they were tossed about by a fierce monsoon in the Bay of Bengal. Ann became desperately ill and Judson expected her death momentarily. Attended only by her husband, Ann gave birth to her first baby, which soon died and was buried at sea. As they sailed into the harbor of Rangoon, Ann finally rallied. Before them lay a squalid, unspeakably filthy village, whose uncivilized life had been utterly untouched and unsoftened by western influence. The night was made terrible by the cries of the dogs and pigs fighting for the garbage littered throughout the village. That night, said Judson in a letter written soon thereafter, "we have marked as the most gloomy and distressing we have ever passed." Instead of rejoicing that at last they had reached a heathen land where they might stay and proclaim the Gospel, they found consolation, he writes, "only in looking beyond our pilgrimage, which we hoped would be short, to that peaceful region where the weary are at rest." Speedy death, either from disease or at the hands of Burma's notoriously cruel officials, seemed to stare them in the face; and they were sorely tempted to return to America, concluding that God had shut the door in their face. But as they prayed through the long vigils of the night, the voice of the Lord comforted them, saying, "Fear not, for I am with thee; be not dismayed, for I am thy God." Assured that their blessed Lord was with them and that their commission was still binding, they determined to go forward, whatever the cost, soothed and sustained by the constraints of divine love. They were:

Assured of their Lord's presence!

Comforted by His promise!

Made strong in His love!

The next morning, July 13, 1813, they disembarked. Look ye mortals! Look ye angels! Look ye ages to come! Behold the scene as these two intrepid souls leave the vessel, thereby committing themselves irrevocably to the dark uncertainties of the future, although Mrs. Judson was still so ill she had to be carried in a stretcher! Behold and weep as they go forth together into the chamber of horrors and the vale of bitter tears!

Then began the third great epoch in Judson's memorable pilgrimage.

III. THE LOVE OF CHRIST GLORIFIED HIS TRIBULATIONS

Following the missionaries in their holy adventure, we behold scenes too horrible for words. On one occasion Judson, pitifully weak and emaciated, was driven in chains across the burning tropical sands. His back lacerated beneath the lash, and his feet covered with blisters, he fell to the ground and prayed that the mercy of God might grant him a speedy death. For almost two years he was incarcerated in a prison too vile to house animals. He was bound with three pairs of chains and his feet were fastened in stocks which, at times, were elevated so that only his shoulders touched the ground. The room into which he and many other prisoners were crowded was without a window and felt like a fiery furnace under the merciless glare of the tropical sun. The stench was terrible; vermin crawled everywhere and the jailer, Mr. Spotted Face, was a brute in human form. Judson saw prisoners dragged out and executed; he lived in terrifying suspense and was able to say with Paul, "I die daily."

Surely he would have fallen and perished under the weight of his cross had it not been for the tender, persistent, beautiful ministrations of Ann. She bribed the jailer as often as possible and then, under cover of darkness, crept to the door of Judson's den bringing food and whispering words of hope and consolation. For three long weeks she did not appear; but, upon her return, bore in her arms a newborn baby that explained her absence. An epidemic of smallpox was raging unchecked through the city, and little Maria was smitten with the dreaded disease. Due to the double strain of concern for her imprisoned husband and the suffering baby, Ann found herself unable to nurse the little one. Tormented by its pitiful cries, Ann took her baby up and down the streets of the city, pleading for mercy and for milk: "You women who have babies, have mercy on my baby and nurse her!"

Near the prison gate was a caged lion, whose fearful bellowing had told all that he was being starved against the day when he would be turned loose upon some of the prisoners. But the lion died of hunger before the plan was executed. Thereupon, plucky Mrs. Judson cleaned out the cage and secured permission for her husband to stay there for a few weeks, since he was critically ill with a fever.

One of the most pathetic pages in the history of Christian missions is that which describes the scene when Judson was finally released and returned to the mission house seeking Ann, who again had failed to visit him for some weeks. As he ambled down the street as fast as his maimed ankles would permit, the tormenting question kept repeating itself, "Is Ann still alive?" Upon reaching the house, the first object to attract his attention was a fat, half-naked Burman woman squatting in the ashes beside a pan of coals holding on her knees an emaciated baby so begrimed with dirt that it did not occur to him that it might be his own. Across the foot of the bed, as though she had fallen there, lay a human figure that, at the first glance, was no more recognizable than his child. The face was ghastly pale and the body was shrunken to the last degree of emaciation. The glossy, black curls had all been shorn from the finely shaped head. There lay the faithful and devoted wife who had followed him so unwearily from prison to prison, ever alleviating his distresses and consoling him in his trials. Presently Ann felt warm tears falling upon her face and, rousing from her stupor, saw Judson by her side.

And there were other sorrows. Before he had been in Burma fourteen years he buried Ann and all of his children. But "the love that never fails" sustained him. "If I had not felt certain," he says, "that every additional trial was ordered by infinite love and mercy, I could not have survived my accumulated sufferings." Judson joined with Paul in declaring: "The love of Christ constraineth me…Therefore I will glory in reproaches, in persecution and in distresses for Christ's sake."

Thus began the fourth epoch in the life of this amazing man, this apostle of the love of Christ in Burma.

IV. THE LOVE OF CHRIST ANIMATED ALL HIS UNDERTAKINGS

Judson had two master passions. One was to translate the Bible into Burmese so that multitudes whom he would never see could read it and hear God's voice speaking directly to their own hearts. Having mastered the intricacies of this very difficult tongue, he spent long days, weary months and exhausting years translating. While engaged in this pursuit, he was dragged away to languish in prison at Ava and Oung-Pen-La. Ruffians were plundering every white man's house. What was to be done to preserve the precious manuscripts? What seemed to be a clever plan occurred to Ann: She would hide the manuscripts in a pillow! Having done this, she brought the pillow to the prison and no one dreamed that the white man's head rested at night on the most precious of treasures—the Word of God.

Then came a crushing misfortune. Taking a fancy to the pillow, the jailer grabbed it and kept it as his own. Judson's spirit groaned within him. What an irreparable loss! But Ann's ingenuity was not yet exhausted. Having made a prettier, nicer pillow, she brought it to the prison and Judson said to the jailer, "How would you like to exchange the old, soiled pillow for this bright new one?" Mr. Spotted Face readily agreed, wondering at the odd taste of the white man. Thus the precious manuscripts were recovered. Many times, smitten down with disease and at death's door, he breathed out the prayer, "Lord, let me finish my work. Spare me long enough to put Thy saving Word into the hands of a perishing people." What a day of rejoicing it was when the Word of God came off the press with its stupendous invitation, "Whosoever will, let him take of the Water of Life freely."

Judson's concern to get the Gospel into the language of other tribes and nations was shared by his wife. Ann was the first missionary to learn Siamese and to translate a portion of Scripture, the Gospel of Matthew, into that tongue.

Judson had a second passion and prayer, namely, to lead individuals to know Christ in His transforming power and to live to see one hundred converts. With great tact and consuming zeal, he preached by the roadside and dealt with inquirers. Years went by without a single convert, but he refused to be discouraged. When a member of the Mission Board in America wrote, deploring the lack of results, and inquired concerning the prospects, this intrepid ambassador of Christ replied, "The prospects are as bright as the promises of God." There were many disappointments, but six years of unwearied effort and fervent supplication were finally rewarded. His Journal of June 27, 1819, gives the thrilling record. "We proceeded," he says, "to a large pond, the bank of which is graced with an enormous image of Buddha, and there administered baptism to Maung Nau, the first Burman convert. Oh, may it prove the beginning of a series of baptisms in the Burman empire, which shall continue in uninterrupted succession to the end of time!"

With a judicious admixture of gentle entreaty and stern warning, he sought one day to point out to a native woman the momentous alternatives that lay before her. Making two divergent marks on the ground, he said, "This leads to eternal life, while this leads to eternal destruction. Will you leave this straight and narrow path drawn by the Saviour's finger for that which leads to everlasting despair? Will you? Will you?"

Many years later this woman, now an earnest and active Christian, said, "Even now I can hear that terribly earnest 'Will you?' coming from the teacher's lips as though it was the voice of God." Yes, the voice of God! Many listened wistfully to the foreigner's preaching, for even their depraved hearts discerned in his message the tender and imperious accents of the voice of God.

The voice of God!

Its tenderness!

Its imperiousness!

Will you heed the tender and imperious accents of the Voice of God?

Judson frequently went on extended preaching trips to villages scattered through the jungles. As Lower Burma is a delta region with innumerable streams, he usually traveled by boat. While living at Amherst, he became exceedingly burdened for the salvation of his boatman. He frequently went to the man's house to converse with him on his favorite theme, the love of Christ. But as soon as Judson left, the man and his wife would scrub the bamboo house to remove the contaminations caused by contact with the foreigner. As they travelled by boat from village to village, Judson had many hours in which to enlighten his unwilling auditor concerning his soul's need and to tell him of the Redeemer's love. When a trip was completed and the man asked for his wages, Judson would say, "Come to the service Sunday morning and I will pay you." Greatly impressed by the missionary's life and passionate concern on his behalf, the man eventually came to appreciate and to appropriate "the riches of love in Christ Jesus." And so it was that the erstwhile depraved and stony-hearted boatman became not only a Christian, but also a very zealous evangelist among his own people.

The desperate need of a perishing people was matched by the love of Christ blazing in the soul of Adoniram Judson. In a letter pleading for missionary reinforcements, he speaks of "the sin of turning a deaf ear to the plaintive cry of millions of immortal beings who, by their darkness and misery, cry day and night, 'Come to our rescue, ye bright sons and daughters of America. Come and save us, for we are sinking into hell!'"

In the year 1828, an event of vast significance took place. Having come in contact with the Karens, a race of wild people living in remote and almost inaccessible jungles, Judson longed for the opportunity of winning a Karen for Christ and thus reaching his race. This opportunity came to him through Ko Tha Byu, a Karen slave sold in Moulmein and bought by a native Christian, who brought him to Judson to be taught and, if possible, evangelized. Ko Tha Byu was a desperate bandit. He had taken part in approximately thirty murders and was a hardened criminal with a vicious nature and an ungovernable temper. Patiently, prayerfully, and lovingly, Judson instructed the wretched, depraved creature, who eventually not only yielded to the transforming power of Christ, but went through the jungles as a flaming evangelist among his people. The hearts of the Karens were remarkably and providentially prepared for the reception of the Gospel message by a tradition prevalent among them to this effect:

> *Long, long ago the Karen elder brother and his young white brother lived close together. God gave each of them a Book of Gold containing all they needed for their salvation, success and happiness. The Karen brother neglected and lost his Book of Gold and so he fell into a wretched type of existence, ignorant and cruelly oppressed by the Burmese. The white brother, however, prized his Golden Book, or Book of God, and so when he sailed away across the oceans, God greatly blessed him. Some day the white brother will return bringing with him God's Book, which, if the Karen people will receive and obey, will bring to them salvation and untold blessings.*

Accordingly, as Ko Tha Byu went on his unwearying preaching tours through the jungles, declaring that the long-looked-for white brother had returned with God's Book, hundreds received the message with gladness.

When a depraved bandit/murderer slave was brought to Judson in 1828, who would have imagined that, a century later, the Christian Karens alone would have many splendid high schools, hundreds of village schools, some 800 self-supporting churches and a Christian constituency of more than 150,000?

> *March 11, Lord's day. Again took the main river. Soon came upon a boat full of men. Their chief, an elderly man, stated that he had already heard much of the Gospel... We went to the shore and spent several hours very delightfully, under the shade of the overhanging trees and the banner of the love of Jesus... The old man went on his way, rejoicing aloud and declaring his resolution to make known the eternal God and the dying love of Jesus, all along the banks of the Yoon-za-len, his native stream.*

> *In these deserts let me labor,*
> *On these mountains let me tell*
> *How He died – The blessed Savior,*
> *To redeem a world from hell.*

> *The banner of the love of Jesus!*
> *The dying love of Jesus!*
> *The redeeming love of the blessed Saviour!*

Answering a communication from a group of missionary candidates in Hamilton, New York, Judson warned of the danger of growing weary in preaching the Gospel and of substituting other activities for the business of winning lost souls. He says:

> *Satan will sympathize with you in the matter and he will present some chapel of ease in which to officiate in your native tongue, some government situation, some professorship or editorship, some literary or scientific*

> *pursuit, some supernumerary translation, or, at least, some system of schools; anything, in a word, that will help you without much surrender of character, to slip out of real missionary work.*

If all missionaries in all lands had shared Judson's passion for souls, his vision of missionary conquest would not now be so far short of realization. In his first tract for the Burmese people, written in 1816, he included this sanguine prediction:

> *About one or at most two hundred years hence the religion of Buddha, of Brahma, of Mohammed and of Rome, together with all other false religions, will disappear and the religion of Christ will pervade the whole world; all quarrels and wars will cease and all the tribes of men will be like a band of mutually loving brothers.*

More than a century and a quarter have passed since that prediction was made. We are hastening toward the termination of the two hundred years of which he spoke and, due to the tremendous increase in population, there are more—vastly more—unreached and unsaved people in heathen lands today than there were when Carey inaugurated the modern missionary movement. Adoniram Judson is still the voice of God, calling us to pray, witness and sacrifice.

By the mercy of God, Judson lived not only to translate the entire Bible into the Burmese tongue, but also to see thousands pass from darkness and death to light and immortality. At the time of his death there were sixty-three churches and seven thousand converts. "In achieving these triumphs," writes Dr. Boreham, "Judson constantly adhered to his favorite theme—the love of Christ." He seemed convinced, as Dr. Wayland intimates, that the whole world could be converted if only each individual could be persuaded that there was a place for him in the divine love.

After eight years of loneliness following the death of Ann, Judson had married Sarah Boardman and, during their eleven years of married life, eight children were born to them, three of whom died at an early age. Upon Sarah's death, Judson returned to his homeland after thirty-three years absence for his only furlough. While at home he married Emily Chubbuck, who returned with him to Burma to share the fervent labors of his closing years.

The year 1850 ushered in the final epoch in the life of this hero of the Cross.

V. THE LOVE OF CHRIST USHERED HIM INTO THE FATHER'S HOUSE

Judson became critically ill in the spring of 1850 and it was believed that his only hope of recovery lay in a long sea voyage. A French barque, the *Aristide Marie*, was scheduled to sail from Moulmein on April 3rd. The stricken missionary was carried on board by his weeping converts. When the ship, after certain delays, sailed several days later, he was accompanied only by Mr. Thomas Ranney, a fellow missionary. On April 12, 1850, Adoniram Judson breathed his last breath and was buried at sea. Meanwhile, Mrs. Judson waited in agonized suspense for four months before learning of her husband's death.

During the last days and weeks of his earthly life, he frequently referred to "the love of Christ"—his favorite theme and chief inspiration. As his eyes kindled and the tears chased each other down his cheeks, he would joyfully exclaim, "Oh, the love of Christ! The wondrous love of Christ! The blessed efficacy of the love of Christ!" One day he said,

> *I have had such views of the loving condescension of Christ and the glories of Heaven, as I believe are seldom granted to mortal men. Oh, the love of Christ! It is the*

secret of life's inspiration and the source of Heaven's bliss.
Oh, the love of Jesus! We cannot understand it now, but
what a beautiful study for eternity!

The love of Christ! The efficacy of the love of Christ! The secret of life's
inspiration! The source of Heaven's bliss! A study for eternity! Oh, the
wondrous love of Christ!

Shortly before his departure to receive "a victor's crown," he expressed pleasure at the prospect of being buried at sea. It afforded, he said, a sense of freedom and expansion, in agreeable contrast with the dark and narrow confines of the grave, to which he had committed the forms of so many whom he had loved. The vast blue ocean, to which his body was committed a few days later, seemed to Adoniram Judson a beautiful symbol of the love of Christ

Boundless in its breadth,
Infinite in its length,
Unfathomable in its depth,
And measureless in its height.

In the exigencies of death, as in the ordeals of life, Ephesians 3:17-19 was uppermost in Judson's mind. The love of Christ cleansed his polluted heart, sanctified his ambitions, glorified his tribulations, animated all his undertakings and transformed the Valley of Shadows into the bursting dawn of eternal day.

ADONIRAM JUDSON

QUESTIONS, TOPICS, AND ASSIGNMENTS
FOR STUDY

1. Note Judson's life text and how the divisions of the chapter grow out of the theme, "the love of Christ."

2. Where was Judson born? Where was he buried?

3. In three words, indicate the three chief characteristics of Judson as a college student.

4. What kind of parents and home did he have?

5. How did he become atheistic?

6. Consider the remarkable circumstances of his conversion.

7. If fear started Judson toward Christ, what led him the rest of the way?

8. What college did Judson attend? What seminary? Do you know any thing of the evangelistic concern and missionary spirit of these institutions today?

9. Suppose you were asked to give a message on the life of Adoniram Judson. What seven dramatic incidents or experiences of his life would you include?

10. Why was Judson so quiet at the table in the Hasseltine home in Bradford? What were Ann's reasons for deciding to go to India?

11. Ethel Daniels Hubbard—*Ann of Ava*, pp. 20-25

12. Note well the facts and significance of the "haystack prayer meeting." How did Judson come in contact with these missionary enthusiasts from Williams college? How was the first foreign missionary society in America formed? R.H. Glover—*Progress of World-Wide Missions*, p. 107.

13. Why didn't the Judsons stay in India? Note the journey in the *Georgianna*.

14. Name the chief religions and some of the main races of Burma.

15. Note well the drama and pathos of the prison experiences of the Judsons.

16. Mark the extraordinary influence of Ann's life upon Judson and upon mission work and history. E.D. Hubbard—*Anna of Ava*. A.T. Pierson—*Miracles of Missions*, Book 1, p. 64.

17. What crushing sorrow came to Judson at Amherst? Hubbard, pp. 234, 235

18. What were Judson's two master passions? Did he live to see them realized?

19. How did Ann outwit the jailor and recover the precious manuscripts?

20. Note the circumstances of his statement, "The prospects are as bright as the promises of God." Continue to make a collection of memorable sayings or missionary mottoes.

21. Have you any comment on the method Judson used to win his boatman to Christ?

22. Who were the Karens? Who was Ko Tha Byu? Can you account for the Karen tradition concerning "the Book of Gold?"

23. What is your reaction to Judson's confidence in Christianity's early and complete triumph? On what factors was his confidence based?

24. Summarize Judson's missionary accomplishments. Additional data in Edward Judson's—*Life of Judson*, p. 552.

25. Observe the phenomenal results among the Karens: over 800 self-supporting churches, etc., among this one race (of many races) in Burma. It would be apropos to discuss indigenous or New Testament methods (Paul's methods) of church establishment, used consistently with such great success in Korea and among the Karens of Burma, and to observe the relative paucity of results on many fields where foreign money has been poured into church buildings, pastors' salaries, evangelists' salaries, with the result that native Christians and churches have never developed spiritually.

26. Mrs. Judson wrote: "I hope no missionary will ever come out here without a wife, as she, in her place, can be equally useful with her husband. I presume that Mrs. Marshman does more good in her mission school than half the ministers in America." Any comment?

27. Who was the first missionary to learn Siamese and to translate a Gospel into that tongue?

28. For material on Buddhism, the dominant religious system of Burma, see J. N. D. Anderson, *The World's Religions*, pp. 118-135, and for material on animistic practices among Jinghpaws and other races of Burma consult the same book, pp. 9-24.

SAMUEL MARSDEN

BEARER OF GLAD TIDINGS IN NEW ZEALAND
AND NEW SOUTH WALES
(1764 – 1838)

In December, 1814, the *Active* dropped anchor at Whangaroa, near the Bay of Islands, New Zealand. Would the missionary dare to land among the thousands of savages who lined the shore? At this very place some time earlier the English ship *Boyd* had anchored. Swarms of fierce natives in war canoes had come offshore and captured it; and, of the crew of seventy people, two women and a boy were sold into slavery while the other sixty-seven were killed and eaten in horrible cannibal orgies. The missionary knew all about this dreadful incident and realized that, if he landed, his life would be in extreme jeopardy. Nevertheless, he did land. He talked with some of the chiefs and mingled among the swarthy natives. Moreover, he spent the night on shore, sleeping in the open among the warriors whose innumerable spears were stuck upright in the ground.

Who was this man with the dauntless heart, and what was the secret of his gallant spirit? He was Samuel Marsden, and the secret of his mountainous courage is to be found in a mountainous text—Luke 2:10. "I was under no apprehension of fear," he says. "We prepared to go ashore to publish for the first time in New Zealand, the glad tidings of the Gospel.

"*Fear not,*" says the text.

"*I was under no apprehension of fear,*" says Marsden.

"*I bring you good tidings,*" says the text.

"*We prepared to publish glad tidings,*" says Marsden.

"*Fear not; for, behold, I bring you good tidings of great joy, which shall be to all people.*"

Like the angel in Luke 2:10, Samuel Marsden was the messenger of a mighty declaration, the bearer of glad [good] tidings of incomparable import, the herald of good news from heaven to earth.

I. HE WAS THE BEARER OF GLAD TIDINGS TO ALL PEOPLE

Samuel Marsden was born at Farsley, Yorkshire, England, July 28, 1764, of pious parents who were attached to the Wesleyan Methodist denomination. After a grammar school education, Samuel joined his uncle, a tradesman at Horsforth, but was not satisfied to follow a business career. Having discovered the sublimities of redeeming grace, he was yearning to devote his life to the Christian ministry so he might make known to others the "glad tidings" so precious to his soul.

He became a student at St. John's College, Cambridge, where he came under the influence of Charles Simeon, a seraphic preacher of impassioned evangelicalism and of missionary outreach. Though bitterly assailed, Simeon's fervent preaching and conversation circles at Cambridge exerted an enormous influence upon successive generations of students through whose lives issued a stream of evangelical doctrine and devotion that reached the very ends of the earth. One of the students thus influenced—at a later date—was the sainted Henry Martyn who, upon reaching India, fell on his knees in a deserted temple and prayed, "Now, my Lord, let me burn out for Thee!"

Under the influence of Charles Simeon's life and ministry, Samuel Marsden came to a profound conviction of the need of all mankind for the saving Gospel and the responsibility of all Christians to "speed away with the message of light to the lands that are lying in darkness and night." When, therefore, he was offered a chaplaincy in what was then designated "His Majesty's Territory of New South Wales," he accepted, convinced that the appointment would enable him to herald in distant dark regions the "glad tidings" which—as his great text expressly declares—"shall be to all people."

II. HE WAS THE BEARER OF GLAD TIDINGS OF SALVATION

Marsden was ordained early in the year 1793 and proceeded to Hull, where he was to take passage in a convict transport—the only conveyance then available for the far, distant colony. "Young as he was," says Dr. Mason Good, "he was remarkable for firmness of principle and intrepidity of spirit, a strong judgment and, above all, a mind stored with knowledge and deeply impressed with religious truth, which promised the happiest results." On April 21 of that year he married Miss Elizabeth Tristan who proved to be a very devoted wife and companion singularly qualified to share his aspirations and to inspire his highest endeavors.

Marsden was aware that the "glad tidings" of which he was a herald had salvation as their object. The angelic voice specifically delineated the content of the "good tidings" by declaring, "Unto you is born a Saviour." This evangelical and evangelistic note was vibrant alike in the announcement of the angelic visitor and in the proclamations that fell from the fervent lips of Samuel Marsden. This is forcibly and beautifully illustrated by an incident that took place on the Isle of Wight. At that time, England and France were at war, and Marsden's ship was waiting at Portsmouth for the arrival of the fleet it was to sail with to New South Wales. During this period of waiting, Marsden preached a sermon in the parish church at Brading on the Isle of Wight. To discover the far-reaching consequences of that sermon, under the operation of the Holy Spirit, it will be instructive to witness a touching incident that took place five years later.

In 1798 Legh Richmond, the recently arrived minister on the Isle of Wight, was called to the bedside of a young woman who had not long to live. Her name was Elizabeth Wallbridge, though she came to be known as "the dairyman's daughter," and the rare loveliness of her Christian piety was a source of wonder to all the islanders. The members of the family were assembled in the room when the minister arrived.

"Oh Sir," said the dairyman's daughter as she looked up at the minister, "I have such a wonderful Saviour. I am in His hands, and I do believe that He will never leave nor forsake me. In this hope I live and in it I wish to die."

"Sir," sobbed the girl's mother, "we were sinful and miserable until dear Betsy—this dear girl—brought Christ Jesus home to her poor father and mother and sister."

"No, dearest mother," said the girl, "say rather, Christ Jesus brought your poor daughter home to tell you what He had already done for her soul and could do for your soul." Then turning to the minister she inquired, "Would you like to know, sir, how this remarkable change in our lives came about?" She began,

> About five years ago Mr. Samuel Marsden, who was about to embark for New South Wales as a chaplain and missionary, was announced to preach at Brading.

Out of curiosity and a desire to show off my new gown, I attended the service. He took as his text, 'Be ye clothed with humility.' When he came to describe the garment of salvation, I felt powerfully aware of the nakedness of my own soul. I looked at the minister, and he seemed to be a messenger sent from heaven to open my eyes. I looked at my gay dress and blushed for shame on account of my pride. I looked at my heart, and it appeared full of iniquity. Mr. Marsden represented Christ as Wisdom; I felt my ignorance. He held Him forth as Righteousness; I was convinced of my own guilt. He proved Him to be Sanctification; I saw only corruption. He proclaimed Him as Redemption; I felt my slavery to sin. He concluded with a fervent plea to sinners to put on Christ and flee from the wrath to come. Oh, sir, I shall rejoice evermore for that day and that dear man's sermon and that I did put on Christ, though I made no outward confession at the time.

"Christ as Wisdom – I felt my ignorance."
"Christ as Righteousness – I was convinced of my guilt."
"Christ as Sanctification – I saw my corruption."
"Christ as Redemption – I felt my slavery to sin."
"I shall forever rejoice for that dear man's sermon and that I did put on Christ."

Some time later the dairyman's daughter passed away, still witnessing for her Lord. "The Lord deals very gently with me," she murmured. "Blessed Jesus, Precious Saviour, His blood cleanses from all sin. His name is Wonderful. Thanks be to God who giveth the victory."

When Samuel Marsden dismissed the service and left the pulpit that Sunday in September, 1793, he knew nothing of how the Spirit of God had used the message to the salvation of Elizabeth Wallbridge. He may have felt discouraged by the lack of visible results. What a joy i⸱   ⸱m, on the day of Christ's appearing, to discover

IT WILL BE?   ⸱y saved as the fruitage of one sermon stressing the

          ⸱gs of salvation. O ministers, Sunday school teachers,

     ⸱nal workers—whatever the text and whatever the occasion—
point people to Christ! Join Samuel Marsden in publishing "glad
tidings" of free, abundant, endless salvation. Then you, too, will
receive a "crown of rejoicing"—the soul winner's crown—on the
day of Christ's appearing.

III. HE WAS THE BEARER OF GLAD TIDINGS OF LIBERTY TO CAPTIVES

Marsden's ship sailed with the fleet on September 30, 1793. His
journal reveals the depression of his spirit as he contrasted the
warm fellowship of devout Christian friends at Cambridge and
the irreligiousness in evidence on a ship bearing convicts to their
distant place of banishment. He writes: "Once I could meet the
people of God and assemble with them in the place of prayer and
praise; but now I hear nothing but oaths and blasphemies." He was
eager to point the crew and the convicts to the Lamb of God and
asked the captain for permission to hold services on board. At first
this was refused, but prayerful persistence eventually won out, and
thereafter Marsden conducted services regularly throughout the
long voyage. His zeal for souls is indicated by the following entry
in his journal:

> *Thursday, December 12, 1793. I have been reading
> of the success of David Brainerd among the Indians of
> North America. How the Lord owned and blessed his
> labors to the conversion of the heathen. The same power
> can effect a change upon those hardened, ungodly sinners
> to whom I am about to carry the words of eternal life.*

When a person goes forth as a missionary, he is conducting a
momentous experiment: He is literally, putting his faith into the

fire to see whether it is gold or stubble. For if he does not witness souls saved, lives transformed, and social evils ameliorated, he is bound to question the adequacy of his Gospel and the validity of his Christ. It was well for Samuel Marsden, and for those to whom he was to minister, that he carried the true Gospel, that he had abounding confidence in its power and that he kept before him the miraculous success of Brainerd among the idolatrous, besotted Indians of the Susquehanna.

In March, 1794, he and Mrs. Marsden settled in Paramatta, near Port Jackson, New South Wales, and entered upon their trying labors. The population consisted almost entirely of criminals banished from England. The state of morals was utterly depraved; oaths, ribaldry and audacious lying were well nigh universal. "I am surrounded," says Marsden, "with evil disposed persons, thieves, adulterers and blasphemers." He was not dismayed by the welter of wickedness that surrounded him; he was persuaded that the message he was privileged to transmit was equal to the needs of the vilest and most depraved. He announced with confidence the "glad tidings" proclaimed by Christ in the synagogue at Nazareth concerning "deliverance to captives." He describes his first Sunday in the colony:

> *I preached the Gospel of deliverance from the captivity of sin…As I was returning home, a young man followed me into the wood and told me how he was distressed for the salvation of his soul. I hope the Lord will have many souls in this place.*

Marsden usually arose about five o'clock and spent the early morning hours in prayer and study. On Sundays he preached first at Sydney then walked fifteen miles to Paramatta to preach again. His preaching was plain, fervent, and very much to the point. In order to arouse a fitting appreciation of the "glad tidings" of deliverance, he laid much emphasis upon man's fallen nature and the tragic realities of sin. This led some to conviction and conversion, while others rejected his message and denounced him bitterly.

One day, while walking along the bank of a river, he saw a convict plunge into the water. Marsden immediately plunged in after him and endeavored to bring him to land. The convict, however, contrived to hold Marsden's head under water and a desperate struggle for life ensued. Eventually Marsden succeeded in getting safely to shore and, also, in dragging the convict with him, whereupon the wretched man, overcome with remorse, confessed his reprehensible design. Having been incensed by the preacher's emphasis upon sin, he had determined upon revenge. He knew that the sight of a drowning man would summon the instant help of one who would defy any danger in the discharge of duty. Accordingly, he had thrown himself into the stream confident of drowning Marsden and then of making good his own escape. This convict came penitently to the Saviour, became a faithful Christian, and zealously made known to others the "glad tidings" of the great deliverance which had so graciously visited his own soul.

IV. MARSDEN WAS THE BEARER OF GLAD TIDINGS OF COMFORT TO THE BROKEN HEARTED

Marsden's plain Gospel of sin and salvation was tempered by a tender solicitude. His capacity to sympathize with others in their suffering was doubtlessly enhanced by certain desolating sorrows that visited his household. Mrs. Marsden took their first-born son, a promising child of two, with her in a gig one day while on a round of calls among the sick and suffering. The child was thrown out of the mother's arms after a sudden jump of the horse and was killed instantly. Another painful stroke was to follow. Determined not to hazard the safety of another child, Mrs. Marsden left her babe at home in the charge of a domestic while she went out to make some necessary calls. The little one strayed unnoticed into the kitchen, fell backwards into a pan of boiling water, and soon died. It was fortunate that the parents knew Him who is the source of all comfort who said that He came "to heal the brokenhearted."

While hating and denouncing sin, Marsden's heart was drawn out in sympathy toward the wretched convicts, especially the women and children. By various methods he sought to alleviate their distresses and to communicate to them the comfort of the Divine Heart. Monsieur Perron, on a mission for the French government, wrote concerning Marsden:

> *He generously interfered on behalf of the poor sufferers in their distresses, established schools for their children and often relieved their necessities; and to the unhappy culprits, banished from their native soil, he ministered alternately exhortation and comfort.*

Marsden was grieved at the forlorn condition of the female convicts who were thrust into frightful immoralities by the current standards of the colony and by the necessity of finding lodging wherever they could. He sought to relieve their hapless plight by the establishment of a suitable home in which they would no longer be exposed to such insidious temptations, and where they could receive Christian instruction. Hundreds of these outcast women came to know the reality of divine comfort through the human comfort extended to them in their wretchedness by Samuel Marsden.

Although he was bitterly maligned by certain officials; his motives impugned; he continued his efforts, eventually gaining the support of his home government along with approval of distinguished Christian philanthropists as William Wilberforce, Elizabeth Fry, and Lord Cambier. With their help, he was able, upon returning to England in 1807, to induce the home government to send out three additional clergymen, three schoolteachers and four men to instruct mechanics and manufacturing. He was introduced to King

George III and received a gift of five Spanish sheep from the King's flock to take to New South Wales. In these and other projects, Marsden was a pioneer in the development of Australia as a great commonwealth.

His transcendent design, however, was always spiritual and the work for which he most deserves to be remembered did not directly concern the colony in which he had so zealously labored. "I believe," he said, "that God has gracious designs toward New South Wales and that His Gospel, taking root there, will spread amongst heathen nations to the glory of His grace." He was thinking particularly of New Zealand and the Friendly Islands, into which no ray of Gospel light had as yet penetrated.

V. HE WAS THE BEARER OF GLAD TIDINGS OF PEACE

New Zealand is the name given to a group of two large and several small islands located just at the Antipodes. The extreme length exceeds 1000 miles and the mean width is 120 miles. The area is about the same as that of Great Britain and Ireland. In 1642 the Dutch navigator Tasman anchored offshore. Several of his men who ventured to land were killed by savages. In 1769 Captain Cook made the first of seven visits to New Zealand. He obtained much information concerning the country and conferred no small benefit on the inhabitants by the seeds, roots and animals he gave as presents. In 1772 Marion du Fresne anchored his two ships in the Bay of Islands. The captain and a boat full of his crew were captured, killed and eaten by the natives. In 1809 sixty-seven members of the *Boyd* crew were killed and eaten at Whangaroa. In 1816 the brig *Agnes*, with fourteen men on board, was stranded at Poverty Bay and all the crew except one were devoured. A whale ship was cast ashore at Wanganui in 1820 and, excepting two persons, all were committed to the ovens and then eaten. Dr. Thompson states:

It is difficult to convey an idea of the terror in which New Zealanders were held in these early days. Sailors groaning under scurvy and in sight of a country covered with vegetables, the specific cure for that dire disease, preferred toothless gums to contact with cannibals. As a deer dreads the tiger, so do all men dread the eaters of men.

The New Zealand Aborigines were the Maoris. Like all Polynesians, they were firm believers in magic, witchcraft, sorcery, and the evil eye. They lived under the cruel and unalterable law of *tabu*, which means that something set apart as sacred is not to be touched. Every calamity was traced to some violation of the tabu and called forth penalties. When a person died it was through the anger of *Whiro* whose tabu had been violated, and commonly the man's family would be stripped of whatever they had. If a canoe upset, it was because *Tawhirimatea* was offended, and the same penalty was exacted. When they were defeated in war it was because *Tu*, the god of war, had been outraged by some infringement of tabus related to him. Dead bodies were tabu. Those persons whose special business it was to officiate in funeral obsequies could not handle food for a designated period of time, so they would gnaw their food from sticks fixed in the ground.

Life was very cheap in New Zealand. The Maoris engaged in war on the slightest provocation. They were cold-blooded and cruel, often obtaining revenge by punishing persons entirely innocent. They would kill, roast and devour men, women and even little children and "glory in their shame." The sick, infirm and aged were heartlessly abandoned to perish. Chastity was rare, if known at all. Conversation was obscene. The people were given to sorcery, murder, cannibalism and indescribable obscenities.

The Maoris differed from other Polynesians in that, besides feasting on enemies slain in battle, they specially fattened slaves for their feasts. A slave girl would be commanded by her master to fetch fuel, light a fire and heat an oven, whereupon she would be knocked in the head, cooked and eaten.

Such were the Maoris – unspeakably degraded and yet a people of superior intelligence. On a number of occasions some of their most enterprising men traversed a thousand miles of water to visit New South Wales. Marsden made friends with them, entertained them in his home and formed the holy resolution to seek the salvation of this race for whom Christ died.

One of Marsden's daughters wrote:

> *My father had sometimes as many as thirty New Zealanders staying in his home. On one occasion a young lad, the nephew of a chief, died, and his uncle immediately made preparation to sacrifice a slave to attend his spirit into the other world. My father was away at the moment and our family was only able to preserve the life of the young New Zealander by hiding him in one of the rooms. When my father returned he reasoned with the chief, who consented to spare the slave's life.*

While in England during 1807 and 1808—on his first and only furlough—Marsden stirred up many in the homeland to a serious concern for the evangelization of New Zealand. The Church Missionary Society and the Methodists were induced to inaugurate plans which eventuated in missionaries being sent out several years later. Since no ordained clergymen from the Church of England were ready to volunteer, it fell to the honor of three consecrated laymen—William Hall, John King and Thomas Kendall—to join with Marsden in opening up New Zealand to the Gospel of peace, peace on earth based on peace within the human heart, peace among men erected on the foundation of "peace through the blood of His cross."

Marsden was at first inclined to believe that the savages had to be somewhat civilized before they would be able to receive the Gospel. He later changed his mind on this point and declared, "Civilization is not necessary before Christianity. You will find civilization follows Christianity more easily than Christianity follows civilization." The Church Missionary Society specifically instructed its missionaries:

> *Do not mistake civilization for conversion. While you rejoice in communicating every other good, think little or nothing done till you see those dead in trespasses and sins quickened together with Christ.*

While returning from England, Marsden became acquainted with a sickly, emaciated New Zealander named Ruatara who happened to be on the same ship. He had been cruelly treated by English sailors who, under delusive promises, had induced him to sail with them to England and then, after having almost worked him to death, had left him in poverty and sickness to get back to his native land as best he could. Marsden nursed him back to health and won his aid in the grand design of Christianizing his people. He kept Ruatara in his home in Paramatta for six months under Christian instruction, then sent him to New Zealand with assurance that he would follow just as soon as possible.

It was not until his arrival in Paramatta following his furlough to England that Marsden learned of the massacre of the crew of the *Boyd* in the harbor of Whangaroa. He could find no captain of a ship adventurous enough to take him and his party to the land of cannibals, so it was that with his own funds he purchased the *Active*, the first of those missionary vessels which, like the *John Williams* and *The Morning Star*, have rendered such splendid service in the cause of Christ.

On November 19, 1814, Marsden embarked with a motley crew of Christians and savages, together with a few horses, cattle, sheep and poultry, and on December 19, landed at the Bay of Islands close to the scene of recent bloodshed and horror. Ruatara was there to meet him. Knowing the ferocity of his people, he did his utmost to persuade his intrepid missionary friend not to land, but Marsden insisted on going ashore, saying: "It is high time to make known the glad tidings in these dark regions of sin and spiritual bondage." In all the annals of heroic enterprise, was there ever a braver deed? As he stepped ashore, a weird scene was enacted. On the hill opposite the landing place a band of naked warriors, armed with clubs and spears, occupied a commanding position. After a pause, a native advanced, flourishing a red mat and crying, "Haromai!" ("Come hither!"). The warriors then advanced. Some of them wore necklaces of teeth from their slaughtered foes, while others were adorned with strings of money they had plundered from foreigners they had murdered on that very beach. Seizing their spears, they brandished them – screaming and yelling with savage fury. Every face was fiercely distorted and every limb employed in the wildest gesticulation. This was their war dance. But their chiefs declared that it meant a welcome to one they considered a friend and a wonder-worker. This latter impression arose in part from the fact that they had never seen a horse. Accordingly, when Marsden brought a horse from the ship, mounted and rode it, the people's amazement knew no bounds.

That night the fearless missionary slept on the ground among the Maori warriors. "I did not sleep much," he says in his journal. As he lay awake that night, there shone in the heavens above him one of the most striking constellations—the Southern Cross. Then there arose another constellation—the Southern Crown, that brilliant diadem of light, as if to assure him of the glorious issue of his labors. He was cheered by the remembrance that—

> *To patient faith the prize is sure*
> *And they who to the end endure*
> *The cross shall wear the crown.*

Christmas Day fell on Sunday. Ruatara had erected a rude pulpit and had called a multitude of people together for a Christian service, the first ever held in New Zealand. The solemn silence was broken as the missionary party sang "Old Hundred." Then Marsden entered the pulpit to preach. What was his text on this historic occasion? He says that he took for his text the angelic announcement made that first Christmas long ago: "Fear not, for behold, I bring you glad tidings of great joy which shall be to all people."

After settling three missionaries on the islands, Marsden returned to New South Wales, but his heart was still in New Zealand. The *Active* often went to New Zealand to take fresh laborers and returned to Paramatta with intelligent young Maoris to be evangelized and trained before being sent back to their people. Marsden made seven missionary journeys to New Zealand, in connection with which he made long tours through the islands. He spent almost a year on one of these trips of evangelization. He often stepped in between fierce, hostile war tribes and made peace between them. But his highest endeavors were directed toward making peace between sinful men and a merciful Saviour.

VI. HE WAS THE BEARER OF GLAD TIDINGS OF GREAT JOY

For years the missionaries had no converts to cheer their difficult labors. They were exposed to great peril amid the internecine conflicts being waged around them and, more than once, had to flee for their lives. Eventually, the saving truth began to find lodgment in savage hearts. Former cannibals became earnest Christians, houses of prayer and worship arose in many places and the "great joy" promised by Marsden's great text became their sweet portion.

Marsden's seventh and last missionary journey through New Zealand was a memorable one. Although 72 years old and bowed with infirmity, he insisted upon visiting his beloved Maoris once more. Wherever he went he was greeted by the Christians with tears of joy, while the heathen population indicated their gladness by firing off muskets and performing their war dance. One old chief sat gazing at him for a long time. When reproved by a bystander for his seeming rudeness, he replied: "Let me alone. Let me take a long last look, for I shall never see again the one by whose lips God sent to me the blessed news of salvation." Thousands came to greet him and he sought, as always, to make known the "glad tidings" of a wondrous redemption. When he was about to re-embark the Maoris carried him on their shoulders to the ship, a distance of 6 miles. As he viewed for the last time the shores of New Zealand and observed the miraculous changes effected by the Gospel, the venerable patriarch exclaimed, "What hath God wrought!"

He returned to Paramatta. Five months later, May 12, 1838, he went to "ever be with the Lord." As he lay dying, someone spoke to him of the hope that is in Christ. In response he murmured, "Precious! Precious! Precious!"

Three years later Bishop Augustus Selwyn arrived to take charge of the work in New Zealand and wrote these words:

> *We see here a whole nation of pagans converted to the faith. Thousands upon thousands of people, young and old, have received new hearts, are offering up their morning and evening prayers daily, are valuing the Word of God above every other gift, and all, in greater or less degree, are bringing forth some fruits of the influence of the Holy Spirit. What a marvelous demonstration of the power of the Gospel.*

On March 1, 1907, the New Zealand governor unveiled a magnificent cross to the honored memory of Samuel Marsden. This type of memorial was suggested by the erection of "The Prayer Book Cross" near the Golden Gate at San Francisco, marking the spot on which Sir Frances Drake's chaplain held the first Protestant service on the Pacific Coast of America. Marsden's cross in New Zealand is of Celtic design and bears the following inscription:

ON CHRISTMAS DAY, 1814
THE FIRST CHRISTIAN SERVICE IN
NEW ZEALAND
WAS HELD ON THIS SPOT
BY THE REV. SAMUEL MARSDEN

His text was the seraphic announcement of Luke 2:10, "Behold, I bring you glad tidings of great joy which shall be to all people."

SAMUEL MARSDEN

QUESTIONS, TOPICS, AND ASSIGNMENTS
FOR STUDY

1. State the significance of Whangaroa, New Zealand, and Paramatta, New South Wales in this chapter. Locate them on a map.

2. What was the primary motive in Marsden's life? Discuss missionary motives. Cite Scripture passages which contain missionary motivation.

A.J. Brown—*The Foreign Missionary*, pp. 13-28

3. In what sense were student days "preparation days"?

4. In what capacity did he serve both his Lord and his country? Why did he accept the position?

5. What was the significance of Marsden's life text in relation to the inhabitants of New Zealand and New South Wales? How was it integrated into his life?

6. How did God honor the message of "glad tidings" in the Wallbridge home?

7. What was Marsden's attitude toward the convicts, his fellow passengers?

8. Describe his efforts in raising the social status of the convicts. Why was he interested in their progress? Discuss the reason for Christ's humanitarian activities.

9. Was Marsden's ministry one of personal evangelism? List examples.

10. How was sorrow etched with "glad tidings of comfort" in the ministry of the Marsdens?

11. What were the needs of the people to whom God sent Marsden?

12. Tabu has been described as "negative magic." For a further study of this interesting and significant aspect of primitive religion, consult the following:

> J. C. Frazer—*The Golden Bough*, Vol. III
> W. D. Howells—*The Heathens*, pp. 25-45

13. Note the significance of the fact that Christian missionaries have been the chief instruments in the banishment or amelioration of so many social evils, including widow burning in India, foot-binding in China, burial alive in the South Sea Islands, the poison ordeal in Africa, and human slavery. For an extensive treatment of this subject: James Dennis—*Christian Missions and Social Progress*.

14. Mark the subtle peril of making social service the primary aim or an end in itself.

15. Note, also, the error of believing that social service and the civilizing process will lead to wholesale evangelization. What Dr. Patton says of Africa is true elsewhere: "It is comparatively easy to convert Africans to Christianity and to establish them against the later introduction of the vices of civilization. It is extremely difficult to Christianize them after they have become viciously civilized." C. H. Patton—*The Lure of Africa*, p. 127.

16. Briefly outline a typical deputation message which Marsden might have given on his furlough in England in regard to the evangelization of New Zealand. What are the chief elements in an effective missionary message?

17. Select a Scripture verse which characterizes God's providence in the incident involving Marsden and Ruatara.

18. What physical memorial was erected to Marsden? Where?

19. Where was his best memorial found?

DAVID LIVINGSTONE

THE PATHFINDER OF AFRICA
(1813 – 1873)

A young Scotsman had come to hear an address by a celebrated missionary. Following his conversion several years earlier, the young man had begun to grapple with the question, "What shall I do with my life?" The Great Commission had come to have a singular hold upon his mind. Its majestic syllables had for him a contemporaneous significance:

> *All power is given unto me in heaven and in earth. Go ye therefore, and make disciples of all nations, baptizing them in the name of the Father, and of the Son, and of the Holy Ghost: Teaching them to observe all things whatsoever I have commanded you: and, lo, I am with you always, even unto the end of the world (Matt. 28:18-20).*

"All authority is given unto me." *The same power is available!*
"Go and evangelize all nations." *The same program is operative!*
"Lo, I am with you." *The same Presence is assured!*

The young Scotsman had completed his medical education, involving two years of study in Glasgow, and was ready for some high call to which he could give his utmost. His eyes fixed upon Robert Moffatt, who was speaking in behalf of his vehement concern for Africa's perishing millions. The depths of his soul rose up to meet the challenge of the missionary, especially that contained in a sentence of twenty words. Those twenty words are historic, used of God to write an amazing history. The twenty words used by Robert Moffatt that epochal day were these:

> *I have sometimes seen, in the morning sun, the smoke of*
> *a thousand villages where no missionary has ever been.*

The picture embodied in these stupendous words captivated his entire being and fired his soul with a passion which only death could quench. He would go to Africa! He would be a forerunner for Christ in the Dark Continent! He would search out the thousand villages, and other thousands, where no missionary had ever been.

This young doctor was David Livingstone. Born in Blantyre, Scotland, March 19, 1813, he became the Pathfinder of Africa.

I. THE PATHFINDER'S VISION OF A FAR-OFF TRAIL

After hearing Robert Moffatt, young Livingstone's mind was haunted by the vision of a distant trail, leading to Cape Town and on to Kuruman, South Africa, thence to the great plain on the north with its teeming villages without the saving Gospel. His favorite passage now spoke to him with new imperiousness. Two commands and a promise stood out in bold relief, as if Christ were speaking directly to him:

> Go!—as a trail-blazer, a pathfinder, a pioneer!
> Evangelize!—do the work of a missionary! And lo, I
> am with you!—Hence you will never be alone, and
> you will have nothing to fear! "That is a promise I
> can rely upon," said Livingstone, "for it is the word
> of a Gentleman of honor."

Shortly thereafter he received appointment under the London Missionary Society. He hurried home to Scotland for a one-day visit with his parents. He revisited the cotton mill there where, beginning at the age of ten, he had worked from six in the morning till six at night, remembering how he had placed a book on a portion of the spinning jenny so he could catch a few sentences in passing. In this way he managed to study Latin and to read a wide variety of books. He recalled a venerable neighbor, David Hogg, who on his deathbed had said to him, "Now, lad, make religion the everyday business of your life, not a thing of fits and starts."

Livingstone's parents were devout Christians and entered heartily into his missionary plan. As they talked together that last evening about the things of Christ and His kingdom, they agreed that the time would come when people of wealth and station would, support missionaries instead of hounds and horses for the chase. Carrying out the family custom, they were up at five the next morning. David read a Scripture selection and led in family prayer. The Scripture he selected was one which tells of the Divine overshadowing and of an Unseen Friend present in every circumstance and on every trail: "The Lord is thy keeper...The Lord shall preserve thee from all evil...The Lord shall preserve thy going out and thy coming in from this time forth, and even for evermore" (Psalm 121:5-8).

A few days later he stood on the deck of an ocean steamer with the open Bible in his hands and a far away look in his eyes. He was dreaming of adding an entire continent to the domain of Christ! Whatever the cost, he would find a path to the heart of Africa so that he, or his successors, might draw Africa up close to the yearning heart of God!

Not only was he a dreamer of noble dreams, he was a person of practical sagacity as well. Often during the long voyage he could be seen standing near the captain asking questions and learning where the ship was on the pathless ocean by observing the moon and stars through certain instruments. "I shall need this knowledge," he said, "to guide me across the pathless deserts and jungles of Africa."

II. THE PATHFINDER'S TRAIL IN THE DESERT

Landing at Algoa, he travelled seven hundred miles by ox-wagon to the Moffatts Kuruman, a piece of desert transformed into a garden of beauty and fruitfulness. After giving the oxen a few days' rest, he continued his journey to Lepelole. The tribe living there called themselves Bakwena, or the People of the Crocodile, their sacred animal. He built a house forthwith and began to study the language. After six months of diligent application, he could converse and preach freely in the Bakwena language. A year after his arrival in Africa, he wrote to his father: "The work of God goes on here notwithstanding all our infirmities. Souls are being gathered continually. Twenty-four were added to the church last month."

Upon his return from a preaching tour, he found that his people had been either killed, captured, or driven away by fierce natives from another tribe. So he travelled north—a two week journey—to Mabotsa. Here lived the Bakhatla, the People of the Monkey, and here he built another house. As he travelled among the villages, crowds of sick, suffering folk frequently besieged his ox-cart, begging the great white doctor to heal them. At night around the village fire, he would sit among the people, listening to tales of mighty exploits of ancient heroes. Then he would stand and tell the story of the greatest Hero of all ages, the story of Jesus coming from heaven to earth to die on the Cross. The wonder of Christ's atonement was much in his thinking and in his preaching. The first song he translated into the native language was, "There Is a Fountain Filled With Blood." One night, while defending the natives against an attack by a wild beast, he broke his finger. Seeing the blood flowing from the injured finger, the people exclaimed: "You saved our lives by wounding yourself. Henceforth our hearts are yours." Telling of the incident in a letter, Livingstone remarked: "I wished that they had felt gratitude for the blood that was shed for their precious souls by Him who was wounded for their transgressions, and had given their hearts to Him."

It was at Mabotsa that Livingstone had his famous encounter with the lion. Lions were numerous in this locality, and the villagers were terrified because, as they said, "The lion, the lord of the night, kills our cattle and sheep even in the daytime." Livingstone knew that if he could kill one of the lions, the others would flee. So, taking his gun and telling the people to bring their spears, he led the villagers on a lion hunt in which he almost lost his life. Seeing an enormous lion behind a bush, he aimed and fired both barrels. While he was reloading, the lion suddenly sprang toward him. He says of this attack, "The lion caught me by the shoulder and we both came to the ground together. Growling horribly, he shook me as a terrier does a rat." Seeing several natives approaching to attack him, the lion sprang upon two of them, biting one in the thigh and the other in the shoulder. But at that moment the bullets the great beast had received took effect and he fell dead. Livingstone had eleven tooth marks as permanent scars and the bone at the top of his left arm was crunched into splinters. The imperfect setting of this bone produced a stiff arm and caused much suffering the rest of his life.

While his arm was healing, he travelled back to Kuruman for a visit with the Moffatts. He had expected to remain a bachelor missionary, but while recuperating at Kuruman he loved and married Moffatt's oldest daughter, Mary. She exchanged one great name for another and honored both.

Another missionary came to Mabotsa, so David and Mary established a new station at Chonuane, and there, with his own hands, he built his third house. One day the chief, Sechele, called all his people together and listened to the white man's message. "This is wonderful," exclaimed the chief. "But my forefathers were living at the same time yours were. How is it that they never heard of the love of God and of Jesus the Saviour? Why did they all pass away into deep darkness?" The chief's words still sound out an indictment against the Christian church, which even now is trifling with our Lord's command to evangelize all nations. No less than three fourths of mankind are now passing out into the terrible darkness of which Sechele spoke so sadly.

Why was the Gospel so slow in coming?

Why did our fathers pass away into deep darkness?

Does not the Lord's command require obedience?

Does not the king's business require haste?

The chief became a very zealous convert and, with his encouragement, the whole village began to attend the mission school. But soon the Livingstones had to move again because the water supply failed. The day after Livingstone had announced that he was moving to Kolobeng, he noticed the people rushing about as busy as ants. They had decided to go to Kolobeng too, for they felt that they could not live without their white friend, who healed their diseases, taught them to read, and told them of a wonderful Saviour.

The country around Kolobeng was full of wild beasts. Standing at the front door of his own house, Livingstone shot a rhinoceros and a buffalo. He taught the people the value of irrigation and helped them in many ways, but what he enjoyed most, he says, was "to preach the unsearchable riches of Christ, for it always warms my own heart and is the great means which God employs for the regeneration of our ruined world."

For several years there was so little rain and the land became so parched the river dried up. They must move again! But where? Livingstone wanted to go to the country of the Makololos, a numerous and famous race hundreds of miles north, but he would have to cross the Kalahari desert, a feat which Sechele warned was impossible for a white man. However, Livingstone crossed it, discovered beautiful Lake Nagami, August 1, 1849, and returned for his family.

The Queen of the Wagon dreaded the prospect of crossing the desert with three children, but she did not complain. On the way they were startled to see one or two of the oxen suddenly drop out of sight, having fallen into a pit dug and covered over by the desert people to catch game for food. There came a portion of the desert where, for three days, they did not see life of any kind—man, bird, or insect. Their water supply was exhausted and nowhere could they find a spring. For four terrible days they were without water, the children moaning and crying of burning thirst. Weakened by these ordeals, the children became very ill, as did also Mrs. Livingstone; thus, they were compelled to return to Kolobeng, where one of the children died.

Livingstone now had to make a great and difficult decision. He loved his family dearly, but he felt it would be cruelly wrong to further risk the lives of his children while in the desert regions; moreover, he believed God was calling him to explore Central Africa's great, unknown recesses. With a very sad heart, he took the family on the long journey to Cape Town where he sent them to England. As he started back on the long, lonely trail to the north, his sorrow was eased by the hope of completing his explorations in two or three years and of finding a suitable site for a mission where he could settle with his family. He did not know the many long years of separation that lay ahead.

III. THE PATHFINDER'S TRAIL OF MANY WATERS

In turning definitely to the work of exploration, Livingstone was not motivated either by a mere love of adventure or a trader's greed for gain. He had a four-fold object:

(1) It was his purpose to find water and suitable locations for missionary work. The vast area in which he had formerly been working was almost devoid of water and quite unpromising from the missionary standpoint. One day a native who had travelled extensively said: "Faraway to the north there is a country full of rivers and of large trees." If that were true, it meant that the unknown areas of Central Africa were inhabited by millions of people for whom Christ died. What a great missionary challenge would thus be brought to light!

(2) It was his object to discover the true nature of Central Africa. At that time the people of England and America believed that Africa was made up largely of one vast desert, stretching all the way from the Kalahari desert in the south to the Sahara desert on the Mediterranean. Livingstone hoped to show—and did—that this view was quite erroneous and that Central Africa was a vast country full of rivers, rich in vegetation, and teeming with people. Moreover, he knew that three great rivers – the Nile, the Congo and the Zambesi —emptied their waters into three separate oceans, and he was lured on by the hope of discovering their sources and thereby opening up a continent to civilization, commerce, and Christianity.

(3) He wanted to find a trail, preferably by water, for communication and trade from the heart of the continent to both the east and west coasts.

(4) He was eager to expose the horrors of the slave trade and to promote means by which to heal what he termed "this open sore of the world."

With these high goals in view, he set out upon the trail of many waters declaring, "I will open a path into the interior or perish."

Although Sekeletu, the chief of the Makololos, knew that the trip to the coast was long, difficult, and full of perils, he sent twenty-seven of his bravest men to bear the luggage and help Nyaka, the doctor. These men set out on this hazardous and tremendous pathfinding simply out of love for the Pathfinder, for he had no money with which to pay for such an expedition. His luggage included some spare clothes, a case of medicines, his Bible, a magic lantern, a small tent, and some instruments for telling latitude and longitude.

They had many harrowing adventures, but finally, after journeying for more than six months by canoe, ox back and on foot, through forests and flooded rivers, in peril from wild beasts and savage men, for 1500 miles of jungles which no white man had ever traversed before, Livingstone and his men came to Loanda on the west coast. He had suffered thirty-one attacks of intermittent fever, had been assailed by huge swarms of fierce mosquitoes, and was reduced to "a bag of bones." Yet he staggered on. "Cannot the love of Christ," he asked, "carry the missionary where the slave trade carries the trader?" He was not a missionary part of the time and something else the rest of the time. He was a missionary all the time, whatever the means he was using, whether healing, teaching, or exploring. "The end of the geographical feat is only the beginning of the missionary enterprise," is an oft-quoted saying of his. His ultimate objective was always to honor his Lord. "I am a missionary, heart and soul," he insisted. "God had an only Son and He was a Missionary. I am a poor imitation, but in this service I hope to live and in it I wish to die." His soul was mastered by the logic of love! "God loved a lost world and gave His only Son to be a missionary. I love a lost world and I am a missionary, heart and soul. In this service I hope to live and in it I wish to die."

At Loanda, Livingstone found a British vessel. The captain said, "You are ill and worn out after these fourteen years of arduous travel. Come with us to England and rest—and see your family again." It was a most inviting prospect, but he could not desert his

Makololo companions who had repeatedly hazarded their lives for him and who, without him, would surely be captured and sold as slaves. Is it not significant that the ship was never heard of again, never reached England?

So after a rest and having secured some beautiful costumes and other presents for his black men, he turned his face again toward the interior. After perilous escapes from crocodiles, hippopotami, and the javelins of hostile savages, Livingstone and his men reached Linyanti, the home of the Makololo, though the Pathfinder himself was nearly deaf from rheumatic fever and almost blind in consequence of being hit on the eye by a forest branch. He was amused to overhear one of his men boasting: "We went on and on till we had finished the whole world." Another, remembering the impression created by the sight of the limitless blue ocean, said: "We kept on marching, believing that what the ancients had told us was true, that the world had no end; but all at once the world said to us, 'I am finished! There is no more of me!'"

Chief Sekeletu was proud of having helped Livingstone. He now sent 120 of his men with him as he set out down the Zambesi River toward the east coast. They came to a forest where lived the tsetse fly so deadly to horses and oxen. Despite a torrential downpour of rain, they took the animals through at night while the tsetse fly slept. One day Livingstone saw five columns of vapor rising far ahead and heard the sound of distant booming. "It is Sounding Smoke," said the Makololo. Livingstone was the first white man who ever saw "Sounding Smoke," a magnificent spectacle twice as large as Niagra Falls. He named it Victoria Falls. Another day a herd of buffalo came charging at him and he escaped by climbing an anthill twenty feet high. Several times each day he got thoroughly soaked crossing streams and marshy places. His bed was a pile of grass. His food often consisted of birdseed, manioc roots, and meal. Even these were often unobtainable and, for days at a time, experienced gnawings of hunger.

On reaching the coast, he found satisfactory work for his men and sailed away to England to see his wife and children again, after a separation of five years. The loneliness of those years and the gladness of meeting are embodied in the following lines written by Mrs. Livingstone:

A hundred thousand welcomes!
How my heart is gushing o'er
With the love and joy and wonder
Thus to see your face once more.
And there's nothing but the gladness
And the love within my heart,
And the hope so sweet and certain
That again we'll never part.

You'll never part me, darling,
There's a promise in your eye;
I may tend you while I'm living,
You may watch me when I die;
And if death but kindly lead me
To the blessed Home on high,
What a hundred thousand welcomes
Will await you in the sky!

While at home he wrote his first book, *Missionary Travels*, made numerous addresses and was the recipient of many honors. His father had passed away, but it was undiluted joy to be with his mother and family again. The happy months sped by, and he again set his face toward the far off trail, accompanied by Mrs. Livingstone and their youngest son. By the time they reached Cape Town, Mrs. Livingstone's health was so bad she went first to Kuruman to see her parents, then back to Scotland, while he continued his explorations. He was rewarded by the discovery of beautiful Lake Nyassa, September 18, 1859. One day he shot two enormous pythons and saw a herd of eight hundred elephants. As they churned along some stream in the launch Livingstone had brought with him from England, savages lurking in the bush—taking him to be one of the hated slave traders—shot poisoned arrows which struck uncomfortably near.

IV. THE PATHFINDER'S TRAIL OF ANGUISH

Livingstone went down to the Zambesi with much joy, knowing that, at last, Mrs. Livingstone was coming to be with him and to make for him a home. But a few weeks later, at Shupanga, she was smitten low with fever and, despite his utmost care, passed away. Long years ago the Master had promised, "You will never be lonely or forsaken, for I am with you!"

"This is the promise of a Gentleman of sacred honor," said Livingstone; "He will keep His word." Had the promise been broken? Was he now forsaken?

He was tempted to think so as he knelt beside that sad and lonely grave under the baobab tree in the African wilderness. The brave man who had endured so many hardships and faced death so many times now wept like a child. "Oh, Mary, my Mary, I loved you when I married you, and the longer I lived with you, the more I loved you! Now I am left alone and forsaken in the world." Alone? Forsaken? Ah, no! As he knelt in prayer, he remembered the word of Him who promised to be with him on every shore and in every experience. "Leave me not! Forsake me not!" cried the brokenhearted man. And, in answer, he heard the whisper of his Unfailing Companion, "Lo, I am with you," and felt around him the tender embrace of the Everlasting Arms.

V. THE PATHFINDER ON THE TRAIL OF SAVAGE CUSTOMS

In the course of his extensive travels, Livingstone came in contact with many strange, and often hideous, customs. While passing through the country of the Baenda-Pezi, or Go-Nakeds, the people appeared quite unashamed in full dress which usually consisted of nothing more than some red juice smeared over the body and a long tobacco pipe suspended from the mouth. A Bakaa child who cut the upper front teeth before the lower was always put to death. The Maravi women were in the habit of piercing the upper lip, gradually enlarging the orifice until a shell could be inserted. Needless to say, the distended upper lip gave them a very unsightly appearance. Known to others as "the duck-billed women," they were considered especially beautiful among their own people. One tribe enhanced their beauty by filing their teeth, while the Batoka tribes accomplished the same by knocking out their upper front teeth at age twelve. As a result, the lower teeth grew very long and bent outwards at the ends, causing the lower lip to protrude in a very uncouth manner.

Various methods of salutation were in vogue among the different tribes. Some would pick up a handful of sand or ashes and rub it on their arms and chest. Others would drum their ribs with their elbows. The people of the Batonga tribe greeted Livingstone by lying on their backs on the ground, rolling from one side to the other, beating their sides with their hands.

Livingstone often heard the heart-rending death wails in connection with funerals. When the natives of Angola and certain other areas turned their eyes toward the future world, their superstitious beliefs almost drove them frantic. They fancied themselves to be the helpless victims of the fickle and malicious, dispositioned and disembodied spirits. Hence they were constantly seeking to appease the departed spirits. Moreover, they believed that death was caused only by witchcraft and could be averted by the use of charms. Among the Barotse and other races, whenever a chief died, a number of his servants were slaughtered to provide attendants in the other world. In Angola, a funeral was an occasion for dancing, feasting, and debauchery. The natives' ambition was to give their friends an expensive funeral with emphasis on food and drink. When on such an occasion, Doctor Livingstone said to a black man, "Why are you intoxicated?" this was the answer, "My mother is dead and I am celebrating."

Among the Batokas, the chiefs vied with each other in exhibiting human skulls as trophies of valor. On one occasion Livingstone saw fifty-four skulls dangling from poles around a chief's house.

Lions were exceedingly numerous because the people made no attempt to kill them. This was due to the common belief that the souls of their chiefs entered the bodies of these great beasts. They even believed that a chief had the power to metamorphose himself into a lion, kill anyone considered his enemy, then return to human form. Consequently, whenever these people saw a lion, they commenced clapping their hands by way of salutation, expressing good will.

In Cassenge and certain other districts, thousands perished every year because of the poison ordeal. If misfortune befell some of the people of a village, perhaps through sickness or lack of success in a hunting expedition, it was believed that someone was practicing witchcraft on them, and the witch doctor was called to "smell out" the guilty party. Having done this by means of his incantations, he gave the accused person a glass of poison to drink. If the person died, which almost invariably happened, he was clearly guilty! Often one person would directly accuse another of using witchcraft to cause harm. Whether directly accused or "smelled out" by the witch doctor, the accused person was often eagerly ready to drink the poison, believing that the ordeal would vindicate his or her innocence.

Livingstone made no attempt to gloss over the horrors of heathenism. Yet, he recognized that these people, however degraded, were among those for whom Christ died. Livingstone unweariedly pointed them to the Lamb of God. He said:

The more intimately I become acquainted with barbarians, the more disgusting does heathenism become. It is lamentable to see those who might be children of God, dwelling in peace and love, so utterly the children of the devil. Oh, Almighty God, help! help! And leave not this wretched people to the slave dealer and Satan. Help them to look to Christ and live.

VI. THE PATHFINDER ON THE TRAIL OF THE SLAVE TRADE

After the death of Mrs. Livingstone at Shupanga, the Pathfinder realized that he was fast nearing the end of his own trail. He dedicated his remaining time and energies to the high task of opposing the traffic in human lives, believing that thereby he would be rendering the largest possible service to Africa and to the cause of Christ. He states in his journal: "I will place no value on anything I possess or anything I may do, except in relation to the Kingdom of Christ."

In 1864 he went to England for his second and last visit. Seeking consolation among his children and arousing the people of Britain to the recognition of their Christian obligation toward the Dark Continent, he stayed in the homeland one year. He should have rested and built up his strength but, instead, spent most of his time interviewing Gladstone (and other notables), delivering speeches exposing the iniquitous slave trade, and writing the book *The Zambesi and Its Tributaries*. A book full of pathetic stories about captured Africans, *Zambesi* told of how Arab and Portuguese slave traders chained and drove their Africans so hard in route to the markets that five out of every six perished along the way from either floggings, starvation, broken heartedness or all three.

Returning to Africa, he walked down to the Zanzibar slave market where he saw three hundred Africans up for sale and three hundred others being brought into town. He could hardly foresee that, not many years after his death and largely through his influence, not only would the slave traffic be abolished, but a beautiful church would be erected on the very site of the Zanzibar slave market.

He started now on his last trail. Every day, when traveling in his launch, he saw corpses floating in the water. Every morning the paddles had to be cleared of dead bodies caught by the floats during the night. Most of the journey was made on foot and, said Livingstone: "Wherever we walk, human skeletons are seen in every direction. This region, which only 18 months ago was a well peopled valley of villages and gardens, is now a desert literally strewn with human bones."

One day he came suddenly upon a long line of men, women, and children chained to one another, with cruel slave sticks fastened around the necks of the men. Slave drivers, carrying muskets, swaggered along beating the captives with whips to make them go faster. Just then the slave traders spied Livingstone and fled pell-mell into the forest. With great rejoicing, he cut the bonds of the women and children, then sawed off the chains and the slave sticks from the men. These people, of whom there were eighty-four, freed first from physical slavery and later from the slavery of sin through faith in Christ, became the first fruits of a great harvest in this section of Africa.

As he traveled deeper into the interior, many hardships befell him. The slave traders had burned hundreds of villages and it was almost impossible to obtain food. "I took up my belt three holes to relieve hunger," he wrote in his journal. Worst of all, one of his men ran off with his precious medicine box. Now he had no quinine with which to fight the ever recurring fever. "This loss," he says, "is like the sentence of death." Ill with fever and half starved, he staggered along the trail till he saw the blue of Lake Tanganyika waters, then on till he discovered Lake Moero and many months later, Lake Bangweola. Sores appeared on his feet. He suffered terribly from dysentery and other ailments causing much loss of blood. All his companions deserted him but three. "Only a ruckle of bones," he finally reached Ujiji to find that all his provisions and goods had been stolen. He felt himself to be the man who was robbed and left helpless on the Jericho Road, but he did not know that the Good Samaritan was close at hand.

One of his men rushed up shouting, "A white man is coming! Look!" Down the village path walked a white man at the head of a caravan of African followers with the flag of the United States unfurled over their heads. It was Henry M. Stanley, happy to find Livingstone at last. Livingstone was very happy, too. This was the first white man he had seen in five years. Moreover, Stanley brought a quantity of wholesome food for him and letters from his children in England.

"How do you come to be in this remote place?" inquired Livingstone. Then Stanley told how, exactly two years before, he had been summoned by James Gordon Bennett of the New York Herald, who said: "Stanley, it is reported that David Livingstone is dead. I do not believe it. He is far away in Central Africa, lost, ill, and stranded. I want you to go and find Livingstone, and give him any help he needs. Never mind the cost. Go and find Livingstone, and bring him back to the civilized world." Such was the commission given by one man to another. And what is our commission, O Christians? In tones of imperious tenderness, our living Lord is saying to us, as He said to Carey and Judson and Livingstone: "Go and find lost men. The cities and plains, the continents and islands, are full of lost people for whom I died. Never mind the cost. Never mind the difficulties. Go and find lost souls and bring them to Me." At tremendous cost and after encountering almost insuperable difficulties, Stanley carried out his commission. What are we doing with ours?

For four months the two men lived together, talked, and traveled. "You have brought me new life," Livingstone repeated again and again; "you are my Good Samaritan." Stanley tried to persuade Livingstone to accompany him to England to see his children. "I must finish my task," the Pathfinder replied. And so, with sad hearts and misty eyes, the two great travelers grasped hands and said, "Farewell." Livingstone was never seen by a white man again.

Stanley was tremendously impressed with Livingstone's character. This is his estimate:

> *For four months I lived with him in the same house or in the same boat or in the same tent, and I never found a fault in him. His gentleness never forsakes him. No harassing anxieties, distraction of mind, long separation from home and kindred, can make him complain. He thinks all will come out right at last; he has such faith in the goodness of Providence.*

Right at last! He had staked everything on the promise, "Lo, I am with you," knowing that this would take care of everything. Will "all come out right at last?" We shall see.

Turning his face toward the hinterland, he set out again on the sad slave trail. On his 59th birthday he made this entry in his journal: "March 19th, birthday. My Jesus, my King, my Life, my All; I again dedicate my whole self to Thee. Accept me and grant, O gracious Father, that ere this year is gone, I may finish my task. In Jesus' name I ask it. Amen, so let it be. David Livingstone."

Not long after this he sent a letter to the *New York Herald*, seeking to secure American help in stamping out the slave trade. He closed his letter with these words which are now to be found on his memorial tablet in Westminster Abbey: "All I can add in my loneliness is, may Heaven's richest blessing come down on every one, American, English, or Turk, who will help to heal this open sore of the world."

Although Livingstone was not successful in his desire to locate the source of the Nile, he deserves to rank as one of the world's greatest explorers. He traveled 29,000 miles in Africa, discovered Victoria Falls and four important lakes (Ngami, Nyassa, Moero, and Bangweola), besides several rivers, and added to the known portion of the world about a million square miles of territory. Yet these accomplishments in themselves were only secondary in his estimation. His all encompassing objective was to open a way for the heralds of redemption and to apply the Gospel to the task of abolishing the slave trade in the name of Him who said: "The spirit of the Lord is upon me, because he hath anointed me to preach the Gospel, to preach deliverance to the captives and to set at liberty them that are bruised."

The Pathfinder became so weak and suffered such agonies of pain, he had to be carried in a stretcher by his remaining black men. At length they came to Chitambo's village where a little hut was built, a rough cot prepared and, early the next morning, May 4, 1873, they found him dead. Two of his servants, Susi and Chumah, took charge of affairs and displayed a devotion which has seldom, if ever, been equaled. His journal, papers and instruments were carefully packed in watertight boxes. The heart of the missionary was buried in the land to which he had given all his heart, while the body, after being embalmed by native methods, was taken on the long march to the coast then sent to England.

On April 18, 1874, accompanied by Henry M. Stanley, his wife's aged father, Robert Moffatt and a great concourse of people, the remains were taken to their final resting place in Westminster Abbey. Thus was accorded to David Livingstone the highest honor which his native land could bestow.

VII. THE PATHFINDER'S COMPANION ON EVERY TRAIL

As a young man, Livingstone saw a vision of "the smoke of a thousand villages where no missionary has ever been" and heard a Voice saying: "Go! Preach the Gospel and explore the unknown continent. Make disciples and open a way for the Gospel." It seemed an impossible assignment, until the Voice added: "You will never be alone and you have nothing to fear. Lo, I am with you all the way." Did the promise hold good? Did the Presence ever fail him?

He was on the bank of the Zambesi River, surrounded by fierce and infuriated savages threatening to kill him. At any moment spears might come hurling through the darkness, or perhaps, a later attack would come at dawn. Opening his tin box and taking out his Bible, he read a precious passage. Let the story be told in his own words as found in his journal:

> *January 14, 1856. See, O Lord, how the heathen rise up against me, as they did to Thy Son. I commit my way unto Thee. 'A guilty, weak, and helpless worm, on Thy kind arms I fall.' Oh Jesus, leave me not, forsake me not!*

The journal contains another entry written that night:

> *Evening. Felt much turmoil of spirit in view of having all my plans for the welfare of this great region knocked on the head by savages tomorrow. But I read that Jesus came and said, 'All power is given unto me in heaven and in earth. Go ye therefore, and teach all nations... and lo, I am with you always, even unto the end of the world.' It is the word of a Gentleman of the most sacred and strictest honor, so there's an end of it. I shall take observations for latitude and longitude tonight, though they may be the last. I feel quite calm now, thank God.*

The words, "Lo, I am with you" are underlined in his journal, because they were first inscribed and underlined in his heart. Later, while on his first visit to the homeland, he was the recipient of the degree of Doctor of Laws at the University of Glasgow and stood before the convocation audience to speak. His body showed all too clearly the evidences of exposure, of privations, and of more than thirty attacks of tropical fever. His left arm , crushed under the lion's teeth, hung stiffly at his side. The great assembly was awed to silence and melted to tears as he related his experiences and then "without misgiving and with gladness of heart. For would you like me to tell you what supported me through all the years of exile among people whose attitude toward me was always uncertain and often hostile? It was this: 'Lo, I am with you always, even unto the end of the world!' On those words I staked everything and they never failed! I was never left alone."

Shadrach, Meshach, and Abednego were not alone in the fiery furnace! Daniel was not alone in the den of lions! Livingstone was not alone when surrounded by infuriated savages! David Livingstone staked everything on the Master's promise. Did it ever fail?

The Pathfinder is sitting in his little hut on the bank of a stream far away in the interior. He is greatly dejected in spirit. His strength has been sapped by many attacks of fever and he wonders if he has much longer to live. His heart bleeds as he sees the depravity of the people around him—forever fighting, plundering, killing, capturing and selling each other into slavery. With their committing such atrocities he is tempted to wonder if the light of the Gospel will ever dawn in their wretched souls. He shudders as he remembers how, just a few hours earlier, the savages had seized two men, and, before his very eyes, had hewn them to pieces with their axes. It seems more than probable that he will be a victim of savage ferocity or cut off by some tropical disease. Something like a moan escapes his lips as he murmurs, "If I only had someone to talk to! Someone who understands! Someone who cares!" Taking his Bible, he reads several favorite passages, then kneels – that being the posture he always assumed in prayer, whether praying in private or with the natives. "Good and gracious Jesus," he prays, "Thou art ever near. Thou knowest my yearnings after these people. Thou art my comfort and my keeper. Stay with me, Lord, till my work is done."

"Thou are ever near." *Someone to talk to!*

"Thou knowest." *Someone who understands!*

"My comfort and my keeper." *Someone who cares!*

"Stay with me." *"Lo, I am with you all the way!"*

Thus accompanied and thus reassured, he continues his labors. "I am immortal," he declares, "till my work is accomplished. And though I see few results, future missionaries will see conversions follow every sermon. May they not forget the pioneers who worked in the thick gloom with few rays to cheer, except such as flow from faith in the precious promises of God's Word."

Did the promise and the Presence ever fail him? At last, weary from long travels, weakened by manifold deprivations, almost famished for lack of food, and broken by disease, David Livingstone lay on a rude cot in Chitambo's village while one of the black men kept watch. Hearing the sound of approaching feet very early in the morning, he inquired, "Whom do you seek and what do you want?" The spokesman replied, "We are seeking the great White Doctor. We have come to urge him to go with us to our village to take away the pain from our sick. May we talk with him?" Peering into the hut, the watcher saw the white man on his knees by the cot. Turning to the delegation he said, "You'll have to wait awhile. The White Doctor is ill. Besides, he is praying to his God and must not be disturbed."

After awhile several weary men appeared from the jungle with the message, "Our chief has sent us a long journey to ask the White Missionary to go again to our tribe to tell us more about Jesus who died for us black people." After peering into the hut, the watcher said, "The White Missionary is praying beside his cot. Let us not disturb him now."

Just at dawn another delegation arrived to report, "We are friends of the White Missionary. Hearing of his illness we have come to see him and to offer our assistance to the one who has helped us in so many ways." Looking again into the hut and seeing his master still on his knees, the watcher—alarmed—called for Susi and Chumah. Entering, they found the Pathfinder on his knees; his soul had departed.

His Lord had promised, "Lo, I am with you all the way, even unto the end." Did the promise fail him at last? Remember, he died on his knees! Was his Lord's presence with him even unto the end? He died in the act of prayer! His last words were praying words. He was not alone! He was talking to Somebody! As he entered the valley of shadows and took the road across the river, David Livingstone was holding sweet converse with the One who was his Unfailing Companion on every shore, in every solitude, and on every trail!

DAVID LIVINGSTONE

QUESTIONS, TOPICS, AND ASSIGNMENTS
FOR STUDY

1. Where was Livingstone born? When and where did he die?

2. Tell of Livingstone's conversion. W. G. Blaikie—*Personal Life of David Livingstone*, pp.28, 29.

3. Livingstone resolved to fulfill his missionary obligation by "giving to missions all he might earn beyond what was required for his subsistence." What changed his mind?

4. What is his famous statement concerning his life text, Matthew 28:20? What does the validity of the promise rest upon?

5. Note carefully Livingstone's study and training both formal and practical. How did he gain valuable knowledge on shipboard?

6. Mark Livingstone's farewell visit to his home, formal devotions, etc. An impromptu dramatization of this scene can be a real blessing in class.

7. What society did Livingstone go out under? Why did he eventually leave this society?

8. How long before Livingstone was able to speak Bakwena fluently?

9. What was the sacred animal of the Bakwena people? This would be an appropriate place to discuss totemism. Bibliography:
    W. Howells—*The Heathens*, pp. 185-201.
    E. D. Soper—*Religions of Mankind*, pp. 64-87.
    A. Goldenweiser—*Early Civilization*, pp. 282-291.

10. One year following Livingstone's arrival in Africa, what were the evidences of divine blessing?

11. What was the sacred animal of the Bakhatla?

12. What was Livingstone's favorite story and song?

13. Note the following results of his encounter with a lion:

      A.   Physical
      B.   Matrimonial

14. Note Sechele's pathetic words. What answer do we have? "Why is the gospel so slow in coming?" Discuss in class. Then would it not be well to *pray*?

15. Name five types of service rendered by Livingstone to the people. Is it wrong for evangelicals to minister to people's physical and earthly needs? What is the danger in so-called social service?

16. Family separation is a problem in missionary life. Were people justified for censuring Livingstone for sending his wife and children to England? Blaikie, pp. 146, 147

17. What were the four great objects of Livingstone's explorations?

18. Mark the perils and sufferings of his journey to Loanda and back, and the incentive or impulse that impelled him.

19. What new name did he give to "Sounding Smoke?"

20. While on furlough in England and Scotland, what book did he write?

21. What was his bitter experience at Shupanga? Did the promise fail him?

22. Enumerate some of the weird customs of the Africans specifically in the areas of:

>   A.   Appearance
>   B.   Modes of salutation
>   C.   Spirits
>   D.   Witchcraft
>   E.   Lions and reincarnation
>   F.   Poison ordeal

23. What other books did Livingstone write?

24. How did Livingstone impress and influence Stanley? Blaikie, pp. 441-443, 448

25. What challenge comes to you as you contemplate Mr. Bennett's commission and Stanley's fidelity in carrying it out? What is our Lord's commission?

26. Cite some crises in which Livingstone's text did not fail.

27. What was done with his heart? His body?

28. The inscription on Livingstone's memorial tablet in Westminster Abbey contains these words: "Brought by faithful hands over land and sea..." Whose hands? Note the remarkable devotion of these two humble Africans, both before and after Livingstone's death.

29. What were the hidings of power (sources of greatness) in Livingstone's life?

30. Note the tremendous impetus to missionary advance produced by Livingstone's life and death:

    A.   Upon missionary volunteers: Alexander Mackay, Mary Slessor and a host of others;

    B.   Upon the churches and Christians generally in the establishment of three new missions to Africa and the extension of the work of two others.

    R.H. Glover—*Progress of World-Wide Missions*, pp. 245, 246.

JAMES CHALMERS

THE GREATHEART OF NEW GUINEA
(1841 – 1901)

The Newly arrived missionary was quickly initiated into the Society of the Heroes of Faith, whose heritage is thus described by its founder: "In journeyings often, in perils of water, in perils of robbers in perils by the heathen, in perils in the wilderness, in perils of the sea; in weariness and painfulness, in watchings often, in hunger and thirst, in fastings often, in cold and nakedness." Such was, for twenty-five years, the constant experience of the ambassador of Christ who had so recently landed on the shores of New Guinea. While standing on the beach close to the water's edge, he heard a frightful noise. Turning around, he saw his house surrounded by a mob of painted, fierce looking savages, armed with spears, clubs and bows and arrows. The leader of the group, with a human jawbone as an armlet and carrying a heavy stone club, rushed at the white man as if to strike him.

"What do you want?" asked the missionary, looking the man in the eye.

"We want tomahawks, knives, hoop-iron and beads. If we don't get them, we will kill you, your wife, the teachers and their wives," was the reply.

"You may kill us," said the white man, "for we never carry arms. But we never give presents to persons who are threatening us.

Remember that we are living among you as friends and have come only to do you good." After making many dire threats, the savages retired to the bush in a surly mood.

At dusk a friendly native crept through the bush to the house and said, "White man, you must get away tonight if you can. You have chance to escape at midnight. Tomorrow morning, when the big star rises, they will murder all of you."

"Are you sure?" he was asked.

"Yes," he replied. "I have just come from their meeting at the chief's house and that is their decision."

A serious conference ensued. "What shall we do?" said the missionary. "Shall we men stay and you women escape, as there is not enough room in the boat for us all?" His brave wife calmly replied, "We have come here to preach the gospel. We will stay, whether we live or die." And the wives of the teachers said, "Let us live together or die together." It was agreed that all would stay. They read the forty-sixth Psalm and knelt in prayer. The missionary wrote later, "We resolved simply to trust Him who alone could care for us." Looking to the One under whose command he served, the missionary prayed: "Lord, when we were thirsty nigh unto death, we heard Thy sweet invitation, 'Come!' Having slaked our thirst upon 'the Water of Life,' we came at Thy bidding to this land to point these wretched people to the same cleansing, refreshing, healing Fountain. Protect us, that we may fulfill the mission on which Thou didst send us."

This missionary was James Chalmers and the text that flowed so easily and inevitably from his impassioned lips was Revelation 22:17.

The Spirit and the Bride say, Come.
And let him that heareth say, Come.
And let him that is athirst come.
And whosoever will, let him take the water of life freely.

I. IN THE TEXT HE HEARD THE SWEET ACCENTS OF THE GREAT INVITATION

James Chalmers was born in Scotland, the land which gave the world such romantic names as Robert Moffatt, David Livingstone, John G. Paton, Sir Walter Scott and Robert Louis Stevenson. His father was a stone mason; it was while he and his wife were living at Ardrishaig, a fishing village on Loch Fyne, twenty-three miles south of Inverary, that James Chalmers was born, August 4, 1841. He spent the early years of his life in this neighborhood. "My first school," he states, "was on the south side of the canal, and I can well remember my mother leading me to the schoolmaster and giving him strict instructions not to spare the rod."

James lived near one of the great lochs of Scotland, and he came to love the sea with a passionate love. He was supremely happy in a boat, or floating on a log or plank, or paddling a raft. In such escapades he had many narrow escapes. He said: "Three times I was carried home supposed to be dead by drowning, and my father used to say, 'You will never die by drowning.'" The remark proved to be prophetic but in a very different sense from anything he then imagined.

James was a great favorite with the Loch Fyne fishermen, and he spent much time with them. Being very eager to go out fishing by himself and not having a boat, he improvised one out of a herring box and sallied forth. He was speedily carried out to sea by the strong current and was rescued with difficulty. He loved danger and did not hesitate on several occasions to plunge into the water, at the risk of his life, in order to rescue a playmate from drowning. These experiences were a foreshadowing of many an adventure in his later life, when he steered a boat full of New Guinea natives through the raging surf or when he navigated the little mission schooner through the tempestuous storms that swept over the great Gulf of Papua.

In November, 1859, two preachers came to Inverary from the North of Ireland to hold a series of evangelistic meetings. Chalmers, now eighteen years of age, was the leader of a group of wild, reckless fellows who determined to break up the meetings. Although it was raining hard, he found a large company of people gathered on the first night. He was much impressed by the enthusiasm and joyfulness with which the people sang. The evangelist who preached that night took as his text, Revelation 22:17—"the Spirit and the Bride say, Come. And let him that heareth say, Come. And let him that is athirst come. And whosoever will, let him take the water of life freely." The words glowed with fire and burned deep into James's soul. He went home that night overwhelmed with conviction of sin and a vision of the loveliness of Christ. A few days later, Mr. Meikle, pastor of the United Presbyterian Church, came to the assistance of the groping boy. As he told of the wonders of divine love and explained the meaning of the words, "The blood of Jesus Christ His Son cleanses us from all sin," young Chalmers came to the Fountain of Life. He says: "I felt that this salvation was for me. I felt that God was speaking to me in His Word and I believed unto salvation."

"*Come!*" said the sweet accents of the Great Invitation.

"*I was thirsty and I came,*" said James Chalmers.

II. IN THE TEXT HE HEARD THE CLARION CALL TO REPEAT THE GREAT INVITATION

Revelation 22:17 not only says, "Come!" It also says, "Let him that heareth say, Come!" The redemptive purpose of Christ includes both salvation and service. He who hears the tender accents of the Great Invitation and comes to the Fountain is to go forth to reiterate the divine entreaty.

Chalmers quickly entered into this sublime realization. Immediately upon his conversion he became the teacher of a Sunday school class and began to address public gatherings, both in the town and in the country. The word "Come!"—the Great Invitation of his great text—was frequently heard upon his fervent lips.

He now remembered an incident which he had almost forgotten. Several years before, at an afternoon class of the Sunday school of the United Presbyterian Church, Mr. Meikle read a stirring letter from a missionary in the Fiji Islands. After reading the letter vividly describing the horrible practices of the savages, the minister said, "Is there a boy here this afternoon who will become a missionary and by-and-by take the gospel to cannibals?" Chalmers made no outward move, but in his heart he had said, "God helping me, I will." This desire—now that he had been born again—came back to him with tremendous force, especially after conversations with Dr. Turner, a veteran missionary from Samoa. After spending eight months working with people in the Glasgow slums, he studied for two years in Cheshunt College, then stayed one year at Highgate where he took special studies, including elementary medicine in Dr. Epps's Homeopathic Hospital.

On October 17, 1865, he was married to Miss Jane Hercus. Having received appointment under the London Missionary Society, they left England on board the *John Williams* (the second vessel bearing his name) on January 4, 1866, bound for Rarotonga, one of the Hervey Islands in the South Seas. By way of Australia, they stirred up the Christians to greater missionary zeal. On the way to Samoa, on January 8, 1867, a disaster overtook them. About midnight the *John Williams* was dashed against the coral reefs of Niue, or Savage Islands, and became a total wreck. Despite great difficulty, the seventy persons on board came safely to land, but nearly all their belongings were either lost or ruined. Mr. and Mrs. Chalmers finally reached Samoa and sailed thence to Rarotonga in a ship owned by the notorious pirate captain Bully Hayes who, coming under the charm of Chalmer's personality, acted the part of a gentleman. Moreover, when Chalmers asked permission to hold religious services on board for the crew, Hayes not only agreed but wanted to make attendance compulsory!

On May 20, 1867, more than sixteen months after leaving England, James Chalmers and his wife arrived at Avarua, on Rarotonga. As he got off the ship a native said to him in pidgin English, "What fellow name belong you?" The reply was, "Chalmers," whereupon the native roared out, "Tamate!" and the people on shore shouted back "Tamate!" This was the nearest approach to the missionary's name the South Sea Islanders could make. It was in this way that Chalmers received the name by which he became known on the island of Rarotonga and later all along the shores of New Guinea.

Rarotonga, then, had a population of about seven thousand. When John Williams began missionary work on Rarotonga, in 1822, the savages were immersed in licentiousness, infanticide, cannibalism and all the cruelties of constant warfare. By the time Chalmers arrived nearly all the people were professing Christians, though many of them exhibited little evidence of real conversion. He entered energetically into the work of the institution John Williams had founded for the purpose of training earnest natives to do missionary work. He did some translation work, started a mission printing press, preached often and visited the natives' homes. Using various methods, everywhere he directed sinners to the Lamb of God.

He labored with great success but he was not satisfied. There were relatively few in Rarotonga who were not Christians. Chalmers wanted to go to some place where Christ was unknown and to sound forth the Great Invitation of divine love to cannibals who would be hearing it for the first time. His heart was set on New Guinea and, after ten years in Rarotonga, he and his wife sailed away, reaching New Guinea in September, 1877. At that time New Guinea was an unknown land, full of terrors, savagery and the fine arts of human degradation. Rev. W. G. Lawes, who had opened up mission work in that land and had spent between three and four years of discouraging labor in the district of Port Moresby, wrote:

> *Cannibalism, in all its hideousness, flourishes on many parts of the coast. Every man is a thief and a liar. The thing of which the men are most proud is the tattooing marks, which mean that the man who is tattooed has shed human blood.*

Now that Australia is commonly called a continent, New Guinea—or Papua, to use the native name—is the largest island in the world. Papua means "crisp-haired." New Guinea is 1,490 miles in length and, at the widest part, 430 miles in breadth. It is six times the size of England and has a range of mountains comparable to the Alps. There are many swamps and the climate is warm and moist. There is a great deal of fever along the coastline. The population of New Guinea is approximately one million. The many different languages add to the difficulties of conducting missionary operations and caused Chalmers to say, "The tower of Babel must have been located in or near New Guinea." Real Papuans have a brown complexion and dark hair.

Chalmers found that, for fear of enemies and for purposes of protection, the people often built their homes in strange places. Some of the villages were built over swamps where the streets were made with large trees and the houses raised on poles fifteen feet high. Many villages were situated over the ocean water some distance from land, and the people went from one house to another by boat. Many of the people who lived inland, even when living on high hills or mountains, built their houses in treetops and were reached by long, shaky ladders.

Each village had a *dubu*, a temple used exclusively by the warriors for purposes of deliberation and for shameful abominations in connections with certain heathen rites. At the end of the *dubu* was a sacred place that housed hideous figures with fish-like bodies and frog-like mouths. The *dubu* was usually several hundred feet long with an aisle down the center and partitions (courts) on either side. Here, skulls—literally hundreds—of men, women, children, crocodiles and wild boar decorated the courts.

War and murder were considered the finest of arts among these people. Disease, sickness and death were accounted for in terms of magic utilized by some human enemy. They knew nothing of malaria, contagion or the hazards of filth; they believed that all such things were caused by an enemy using sorcery and it was the duty of friends to see to it that punishment was meted out; They would follow the night firefly believing that its course of flight pointed in the direction of the enemy, or they would secure the assistance of a sorcerer who would pronounce a neighboring village guilty, whereupon they would stealthily attack the village, kill some of the people and bring back their heads. Many tribes were not only head-hunters but also cannibals. "When we first landed," writes Chalmers in one of his books, "the natives lived only to fight and the victory was celebrated by cannibal feasts in which the bodies of their enemies were eaten." He was pained to discover that the natives of New Guinea showed very little skill in anything aside from manufacturing weapons used to fight and kill. The most ingenious of these was known as "the man-catcher." This weapon consisted of a long pole with a loop of rattan at the end. The remarkable feature of the weapon was the deadly spike inserted in the upper part of the long pole. The modus operandi is as follows: the loop is thrown over the unhappy wretch who is in full retreat and a vigorous pull from the brawny arm of the cruel captor jerks the victim upon the spike, penetrating the body at the base of the brain.

The people did not believe Chalmers when told he had come simply to tell them of the love of the Saviour who graciously invites all men, however sinful or degraded, to come to Him for forgiveness and life everlasting. What they thought to be his real reason for coming was indicated in the following conversation which took place between the natives and Chalmers shortly after his arrival:

> "What is the name of your country?"
> "Beritani—Britain."
> "Why did you leave your country?"
> "To teach you and to tell you of the great loving Spirit who loves us all."
> "Have you coconuts in your country?"
> "No."
> "Have you yams?"
> "No."
> "Have you taro?"
> "No."
> "Have you sago?"
> "No."
> "Have you plenty of tomahawks and hoop-iron?"
> "Yes, in great abundance."
> "We understand, now, why you have come. You have nothing to eat in Beritani, but you have plenty of tomahawks and hoop-iron with which to buy food wherever you can find it."

Chalmers closed this account by saying:

> *It was useless to tell them we had plenty of food different*
> *from theirs, and that want of food did not send us away*

from Beritani. We had no coconuts, yams, taro, or sago, and who could live without these? Seeing us opening canned meat, they came to the conclusion that we too were cannibals who had human flesh cooked in our country and sent out to us in cans.

Such were the savages to whom Chalmers had come. And what was the message with which he expected to reach them and change their lives? The following incident will furnish the answer. When he was a student at Cheshunt College, Chalmers received a copy of a book by the college president, Dr. Reynolds. In his letter acknowledging the gift, Chalmers recalls some of the blessed experiences of college days and says: "I have been listening to you again and again as I have read your book and have been drinking in new life from the Water of Life flowing through you."

It was the old, old text! The text that was used to inspire his conversion! The text that led him to Rarotonga and New Guinea! The text whose imagery filled his mind! The text whose message flooded his heart! "Come and take the Water of Life freely."

III. IN THE TEXT HE FOUND THE DIVINE ANSWER TO THE THIRSTINGS OF THE SOUL

Rudyard Kipling has told of the old lama who, for many years, tramped unweariedly across the burning plains of India asking one everlasting question: "Where is the river of which I have heard? Where is the river whose waters can cleanse from sin and satisfy the thirst of the human soul?" Looking at this old lama, the missionary-minded Christian sees, not one man, but hundreds of millions who are famishing for that Water which alone can quench the thirstings of their souls. Chalmers was convinced that the New Guinea savages were just as thirsty as he had been, and that the same Water—the Water of Life—that had so marvelously satisfied his soul at Inverary long ago, would likewise satisfy theirs.

As the site of their first home in New Guinea, Mr. and Mrs. Chalmers selected Suau (or Stacey Island) where they found themselves surrounded by masses of cannibals wearing necklaces of human bones. While the mission house was being built, they accepted the rude hospitality of a chief who seemed friendly but who was, more than once, party of a plot to kill them. They lived in a small room separate from the rest of the house, where they slept on a mattress on the floor. The many human skulls adorning the walls were mute reminders of past victories and of cannibal orgies. After some weeks they moved into their own house and the natives came in droves to visit them—partly out of curiosity and partly to steal everything they could lay their hands on. Some of the savages invited them to eat in their homes. "We received numerous invitations to feasts," says Chalmers, "some of which were cannibal feasts." One day when Mrs. Chalmers was recuperating from a severe illness, a native brought her a dish saying, "Here is something especially nice for you. It will make you strong and healthy." When she exercised caution and insisted on knowing what the dish contained, she learned that it was some cooked human flesh. Chalmers was offered a chief's daughter in marriage and was told that he would never be a great chief if he continued to have only one wife.

In the spring of 1878 Tamate sailed along the coast from east to west in the *Ellengowan*, visiting one hundred and five villages, of which ninety had never before seen a white man. He made extended journeys inland, either on foot or by canoe, following the course of winding streams. Like John Coleridge Patteson and other pioneer missionaries, he always went unarmed, knowing that this would allay native suspicions and, at the same time, leave him defenseless against attack.

The pattern of life was woven out of diverse experiences—some comical, some bizarre, some perilous. He would sit down on a stone, knowing that although no persons were in sight, hundreds of women, children and armed men were in the bush watching his every move. At length an old woman would venture near. Pointing at his boots she would say, "How is it that, although you have a white face, your feet are black and you have no toes?" He would take off one of his boots and the woman rushed off screaming. After a while the natives mustered enough courage to approach. He would shut and open his umbrella as shouts of amazement were heard on every side. When he struck a match the shouts redoubled. He would show them his bare arms, chest and legs, and they wonderingly concluded that he was white all over. In such ways, he accomplished his purpose of making friends with the savages.

He found the Papuans to be extremely fond of pigs, especially when roasted, but it astonished him to find the skulls of dead pigs hanging in their houses and to see a woman nursing her baby at one breast and a young pig at the other.

One afternoon while on the floor in front of the fire inside a native hut, he busily traced his journey on his chart until he became aware of some large, foul smelling drops falling around and on him.

Looking up, he saw a bulky bundle hanging from the roof. "What is that?" he inquired. The native explained that his grandmother had recently died and that he had hung her remains right above the fire so they would be thoroughly smoked and dried. "It spoiled my dinner," says Tamate.

Facing death was a commonplace affair for the Greatheart of New Guinea. The hairbreadth escapes of his early years in Scotland were now reenacted on a much more stupendous and exciting scale. On one of his voyages in the little mission vessel, he came to a bay not seen before by him. As soon as his canoe touched the beach, he was surrounded by a crowd of fierce looking savages armed with clubs and spears. Followed by a mate of the vessel, he made his way along the beach, accompanied by the hostile Papuans till he reached the chief's house. The old dignitary sat on an elevated platform in front of his house and completely ignored his visitors. When Tamate offered him some presents, he threw them back in his face. Taking their cue from the surly, menacing attitude of the chief, the dark mob began to threaten the white man who now started back toward the beach. The crowd followed close on his heels, growling savagely and urging each other to strike the first blow. A man with a stone-headed club was walking immediately behind Tamate and making menacing gestures. Several times Tamate looked around to find the man's club raised to strike. "I must have that club," said he to himself, "or that club will have me." Wheeling suddenly around, he took out of his satchel a piece of hoop-iron and held it before the savage. The man's eyes glistened as if he was being offered a bar of gold. Just as he stretched out his hand to grasp the prize, Tamate seized the man's club, wrenched it out of his hand, and then proceeded to the boat without further molestation.

Before commencing his first long journey in the spring of 1878, Tamate urged his wife to accompany him. She, however, insisted on staying at the station believing that the work would suffer if she, too, were away and that the Rarotonga teachers might sicken and die. One of the noblest, most self-denying decisions in the annals of nineteenth century missions was that of Mrs. Chalmers. Her only helpers were three Rarotongan teachers and their wives. They all were at the mercy of the savages who coveted their possessions and would have considered their bodies as choice dainties for a cannibal feast. Her courage was heroic, but the strain of those early months of constant peril and the anxiety occasioned by her husband's long absence on a very dangerous mission weakened her constitution and made her more susceptible to the ravages of fever. In October, 1878, she went to Sydney, Australia, seeking an improvement in health, but in February, 1879, she finished her earthly course. In the hour of this devastating bereavement Tamate wrote in his diary, "Oh, to dwell at His cross and to abound in blessed sympathy with His great work! I want the heathen for Christ!"

Did Mrs. Chalmers labor and lay down her life in a fruitless quest? Was Tamate wasting his extraordinary abilities and magnificent manhood in hazardous enterprises from which would flow no commensurate results? Was he wrong in believing that the Gospel is the divinely adequate answer to the uttermost need of every human soul and that even savage hearts yearn for the Water of Life?

He tells of a "rainmaker" named Kone who listened attentively to the Gospel message and declared that his heart responded to its appeal. At the man's urgent request, Greatheart taught him this simple prayer, "Great Spirit of Love, give me light and save me for Jesus' sake." When he returned to this district some months later, he found that the rainmaker was dead. His heart was deeply moved as he learned the circumstances connected with his death. The rainmaker was in the company of two Naara men when the chief of the hostile Lolo tribe came stealthily to attack them with spears. The chief threw a spear which would have killed one of the Naara men, but the rainmaker stepped in front of him and received the spear in his own body, thus saving the other by his own death. And as he lay dying, he was heard to pray again and again, "Great Spirit of Love, I come to Thee; save me for Jesus' sake."

"I want the heathen for Christ!" sobs the bereaved missionary.

"Great Spirit of Love, I come to Thee," prays the dying rainmaker.

"Let Him that is athirst come," urges the mighty text.

IV. IN THE TEXT HE FOUND FREE ACCESS TO LIFE ABUNDANT

The great evangelical invitation of the Old Testament is, "Ho, every one that thirsteth, come to the waters…without money and without price." That is precisely the message of Greatheart's text: "Come…take the Water of Life freely without a present, with nothing to offer in compensation." His soul was thrilled with the glad announcement that even those who are clad in the rags of savagery and cannibalism can partake of God's bounty freely.

"God's bounty," be it observed. The Water of Life is a Person—the One who affirmed, "The water that I give…shall be a well of water springing up into everlasting life." The announcement that captured Chalmers's heart at Inverary and captivated his redeemed personality ever after was not: "Come and take one quaff from a half-filled flask." It was rather this: "Come—without money, without merit—and drink evermore of the unfailing spring, the gushing fountain, the artesian well of the Water of Life."

> *I heard the voice of Jesus say,*
> *'Behold, I freely give*
> *The living water; thirsty one,*
> *Stoop down, and drink and live!'*
> *I came to Jesus and I drank*
> *Of that life giving stream;*
> *My thirst was quenched, my soul revived,*
> *And now I live in Him.*

"And now I live in Him." What a magnificent, winsome, heroic life James Chalmers lived in His Lord. Under the spell of his Christian personality the pirate, Bully Hayes, was subdued, men of culture were enamored and savages tamed. Having spent several weeks on shipboard with Chalmers, Robert Louis Stevenson wrote, "He took me fairly by storm for the most attractive, simple, brave and interesting man in the whole Pacific." And when someone asked Manurewa, the chief of Suau, what influenced him and his people to give up their cannibalistic practices, the old chief straightened up, clinched his hands and replied, "Tamate said, 'You must give up cannibalism' and we did."

One day Chalmers and a native teacher found themselves surrounded and followed by a crowd of armed, threatening Papuans. When about two miles from Mailu, where their boat was awaiting them, they came upon another group of people, all of whom—including even the women—were armed with spears and clubs. All that day two groups of savages had hounded their steps for the avowed purpose of killing them. It was agreed that their belongings would go to the natives of Aroma and their bodies to the people of Toulon to be eaten. Tamate's account of this episode is, at this point, particularly vivid and revealing. He says:

> *The teacher heard them discussing as to the best place for the attack. I said to him, 'What are they saying?' He replied, 'They are saying they intend to kill us. Let us kneel down and pray.' 'No, no!' I replied, 'let us walk and pray,' and strode resolutely forward.*

Presently, two savages with clubs came forward and walked right at Tamate's heels. One blow and all would be over. But an Invisible Hand intervened, and at last they managed to reach their boat and escape.

Tamate moved from Suau to Port Moresby, because the latter was more centrally located. He spent all his time trying to make friends with savage tribes and settling native teachers in villages all along the coast. A glance at the work in Suau will reveal the sort of change that was taking place in many districts and that the Gospel light was breaking in upon the long, dark night of heathenism. Before Chalmers landed at Suau in the fall of 1877, the natives came out to the vessel and gleefully told him that they had recently killed and eaten ten of their enemies from a neighboring tribe. On all sides there was gross darkness, bloodshed and cruelty. In 1882 Chalmers found the cannibal ovens unused. People who formerly thought every sound at night meant the coming of enemies, now slept in peace, and tribes that never met except to fight, now sat side by side in the church worshiping the true God. What were the means used to accomplish these results? The answer given by Tamate himself is this, "The first missionaries landed not only to preach the Gospel of divine love but also to live it." Few men have preached and lived the Gospel as effectively as Chalmers. He was a sermon in shoes; he was an incarnation of Revelation 22:17.

Greatheart had as helpers a number of South Sea Islanders who drank daily and deeply of the Water of Life and exhibited to a remarkable degree the fullness of life available in Christ. Many of these he had led to Christ and trained himself during his ten years in Rarotonga. Many of them died of fever, others died as martyrs, but there were always volunteers ready to take the place of those who had fallen. In 1878 the *John Williams* came on one of her numerous trips bringing teachers from Polynesia. As they drew near the shore, a crew member began to tell about the centipedes, serpents, diseases and other dangers that lay before them.

"Wait!" said a teacher from the Loyalty Islands. "Are there people there?"

"Yes, but they are horrible cannibals who will probably kill and eat all of you."

"Never mind," rejoined the teacher. "Wherever there are people, precious souls for whom Christ died, there missionaries must go."

During Chalmers's years of service more than two hundred of these native workers from Rarotonga, Samoa and other far distant Polynesian Isles left all for Christ's sake to take the Great Invitation to the dark hearts of New Guinea. About half of these either died of disease or perished at the hands of the savages. Chalmers called these native missionaries "the true heroes and heroines of the nineteenth century."

Two members of this noble company were Aruadaera and Aruako. The former was a deacon, the latter a teacher. Both were zealous evangelists. They accompanied Tamate in the fall of 1883 on a hazardous trip among the cannibals of the Orokolo and Maipua districts. At five o'clock, October 15, they reached Maipua, "a horrible hole in the middle of a swamp with miles of swamp all around." The leading chief, Ipaivaitani, invited the missionary party to stay in the dubu. Tamate then had his "breakfast and dinner all in one." "I could have enjoyed it better," he relates, "if there had not been so many skulls in a heap close by."

At sunset, a large crowd assembled and Aruadaera commenced to preach with Aruako to follow later. What a weird scene! A large temple, lit only by flickering fires; a crowd of real cannibals who pronounce man to be the best of all flesh; hundreds of human skulls for decorations, and in the sacred place six Kanibus, or idols, holding the power of life and death, of war and peace within themselves. "In the center of this weird crowd," to use Tamate's own words, "sit Aruako and Aruadaera, until recently wild savages themselves, preaching Christ as the revealer of God's love and the Saviour of sinful man." When Tamate fell asleep the service still continued. Upon awaking soon after sunrise the next morning, he found the two preachers still talking, still hearing and answering the people's questions. Aruako in particular had become quite hoarse. "Aruako," inquired Tamate, "have you been at it all night?" "Yes," he answered, "all night. But I can't quit now. After telling them all about the Garden of Eden, the flood and the Old Testament, I have now come to Jesus Christ and I must tell them all about Him." How long would it take to proclaim the Saviour's love "to every creature," if even one-tenth of the professing Christians of America had that kind of zeal?

Tamate closed his account of this beautiful incident by saying, "Yes, my friend had reached Him to whom we all must come."

Come…thirsty ones…and take the Water of Life freely."
Tamate had come and drunk deeply at the fountain.
Aruako had come and found life in abundance.
"Christ is the One to whom we all must come.

When Greatheart was living in Rarotonga he met Anederea, a young man who was living a vile, reckless life. He marked him out as a trophy for Christ and eventually won him. Anederea became a very earnest worker and was one of the first band of twelve teachers who landed on New Guinea in 1872. He soon distinguished himself by his zeal in learning the language of Kerepuna, where he was located, and in seeking the salvation of the natives. In March, 1881, Taria, the teacher located at Hula, along with five Hula boys, went in a boat to Kerepuna and Kalo to bring the teachers and their families to Hula, on account of the serious ill health of some of the party. When the boat with fifteen persons aboard was at Kalo, a large crowd of armed natives assembled on the beach. The chief, named Quaipo, pretending to be friendly, stepped into the boat. After a brief conversation, he jumped out of the boat onto the beach. This was the prearranged signal for attack. Instantly a cloud of spears flew toward the mission party. Four spears struck Taria and ended his life. Anederea and Materua were soon dispatched. A single spear slew both mother and babe in the case of both wives. Four Hula boys jumped into the water and managed to swim to safety, but the other eleven persons were slain.

When the news of this atrocity reached the Christians in Polynesia, a whole boatload of volunteers came to take their places. Chalmers asked a man named Pau and his wife if they would settle at Kalo, where the recent massacre took place. They readily agreed, and he went with them to help them get located. He decided to spend the first night with them, for he was not willing to subject them to hazards which he would not share. It was a daring thing to do. Quaipo had sent him word that he was determined to have his head. Chalmers writes, "We were quite at their mercy, being unarmed and in an unprotected house. Had they attacked us, we should all have been killed." What was his reliance in such an hour as this?" "After evening prayers," he states, "I was soon sound asleep."

> "*After evening prayers*" his heart was reassured.
> "*After evening prayers*" he knew that he was not alone.
> "*After evening prayers*" he fell sound asleep.
> And on the next day he wrote in his diary, "May He who protected us soon become known to them all."

Tamate and his noble helpers found that the Water of Life not only quenched their thirst, but also filled and flooded their lives even unto overflowing. Though quite oblivious of it themselves, they were living demonstrations of the truth which Jesus declared, "He that believeth on me, from within him shall flow rivers of living water." They found that Revelation 22:17 provides both for the imports of the soul unto salvation and for the exports of the soul unto the redemption of others who are famished and perishing.

V. IN THE TEXT HE HEARD THE UNIVERSAL OFFER OF DIVINE MERCY

The bounteous provisions of Revelation 22:17 are not offered to a limited few. Its privileges are not restricted by any racial, cultural or geographical qualifications.

The "whosoever will" of Revelation 22:17 clearly implies that the whole world needs the Gospel, for God would not offer to all that which is not needed by all. The Greatheart of New Guinea labored under the passionate conviction that all men supremely needed the message he brought and that no one who came with a contrite spirit would be turned away.

In the summer of 1886 Chalmers returned to England for his first furlough, after twenty years of missionary service. Wherever he went he attracted and stirred great audiences with his fiery enthusiasm and his story of thrilling adventures for Christ. His messages were utterly devoid of anything suggesting self-pity. He insisted that the word "sacrifice" has no place in a Christian's vocabulary, at least when referring to his own labors. He was engaged in the highest and holiest business on earth and he was radiantly happy. "Recall my period of more than twenty years of service," he said; "give me back all its experiences—its shipwrecks, its frequent occasions on the brink of death; give it to me surrounded by savages with spears and clubs; give it to me again with spears flying about me, with the club knocking me to the ground, and I will still be your missionary."

It was a sweet joy to visit his early home at Inverary with its familiar scenes and, in particular, to kneel in a prayer of thanksgiving in the church where, that rainy night long ago, he heard for the first time the majestic syllables of Revelation 22:17.

While in the homel, three important events took place: he wrote a missionary book, *Pioneering in New Guinea*; he was engaged to Sarah Eliza Harrison; and he declined an urgent invitation to return to New Guinea in the capacity of a government official. Like David Livingstone, Chalmers was "first and last a missionary." At a mass meeting in Exeter Hall, London, he declared:

> *Gospel and commerce, yes; but remember this: It must be the Gospel first. Wherever there has been the slightest spark of civilization in the Southern Seas it has been because the Gospel has been preached there. The ramparts of heathenism can only be stormed by those who carry the cross.*

In the fall of 1887 he returned to New Guinea. He was saddened to learn of the martyrdom of one of his best native evangelists— Tauraki from Samoa. His wife recovered, but Tauraki himself, his child and five friendly natives were killed when a barrage of arrows was loosed at them by hostile Papuans.

In 1888 Tamate met Sarah Eliza Harrison at Cooktown, where they were married, and he took her to Motumotu, which he had determined upon as his new headquarters. The house, which at first had not a chair, bed or table, was lively with rats, cockroaches, spiders, lizards, ants and mosquitoes. They were living among people who were as fierce as they were depraved. In this district they practiced a horrible custom called "biting off the nose." When an enemy was killed there was a rush to see who would have the honor of biting off and swallowing the dead man's nose. When the warriors returned home with several dead bodies the women came out to meet them calling out, "Who are the killers?" After being told, they applauded them heartily. Then they would call out, "Who are the nose-eaters?" When these were pointed out, the women would applaud and honor them even more than the actual killers.

Mrs. Chalmers was a woman of remarkable devotion to duty and a worthy helpmeet for her famous husband. She never thought of complaining, when, on numerous occasions, she was left alone among these savages for many weeks at a time, with the nearest white person 170 miles away. While Tamate was facing death daily as he sought out new tribes in order to invite "whosoever will" to the Water of Life, she was seeking to point the cannibals of Motumotu to the same Blessed Fountain. One day she noticed the house was surrounded by about twenty-five warriors. She was terrified but with a prayer in her heart she disarmed them of any evil designs by boldly going out among them and engaging in a friendly conversation. A school was soon started, in which the children from various tribes were taught to read and write in five different languages. Several native teachers assisted her.

Despite various precautions she often fell prey to the fever germs. The natives had many unsanitary practices. Among these was the very unhygienic habit of burying their dead quite close to the houses. Mrs. Chalmers also suffered from sunstroke. But she refused to be despondent and her indomitable spirit rose above every trial. She was an inspiration to her husband and a great help to the native teachers, who, in times of illness, were inclined to lose all hope of recovery. "We shall die like the others," they would say and would not take medicine unless she or Tamate was there to insist upon it.

Mrs. Chalmers accompanied Tamate on a boat trip to Moveave. There was an abundance of crocodiles in the stream and parrots of brilliant plumage in the trees. Traveling part of the way on foot they found it almost unbearably hot in the bush until they were refreshed by the cool milk of some fresh coconuts. Tamate had visited Moveave frequently and had made friends with the old chief. Upon reaching the town he found that the old chief had died and been buried in front of his house in a temporary enclosure nine feet square. Inside this, according to custom, the whole family—widow, children and grandchildren—had to cook, eat and sleep for several months. The widow, daubed with mud, looked wretched and filthy. She was not permitted to wash during the three months of her mourning. As the missionary party entered the village, the people crowded around them. Suddenly there was a wild outcry and the savages began to make dire threats. There was a great display of clubs, spears, bows and arrows, and the missionaries and their party had a very narrow escape from a general massacre.

In 1890 Mrs. Chalmers's health was so precarious that a change and rest were deemed imperative, so Greatheart decided to take her on a trip to Samoa and Rarotonga. They went by way of Australia where he sought to raise money for a steam launch with which to carry on his missionary expeditions more effectively. As fellow passengers on the boat from Sydney to Samoa, Tamate and Robert Louis Stevenson began an acquaintance which ripened into a very warm friendship. Before going to Samoa, Stevenson had "a great prejudice against missions," but his views were soon changed. "Those who debilitate against missions," he stated, "have only one thing to do—to come and see them on the spot."

Writing to his mother Stevenson said, "Tamate is a man nobody can see and not love. He has his faults like the rest of us but he is as big as a church." Much of admiration and of soul aspiration is indicated by the following extracts from a letter of his to Chalmers: "I count it a privilege and a benefit to have met you. But, O Tamate, if I had met you when I was a youth, how different my life would have been!"

In Samoa and Rarotonga Chalmers moved the Christians to new missionary devotion by telling them of the heroic labors of their comrades and secured many new volunteers for service in New Guinea. Mr. and Mrs. Chalmers returned to Motumotu in July, 1891. Some time later, while he was on the way to Cooktown on the *Harrier*, the ship struck a rock and was destroyed. This was his fourth shipwreck experience.

One day the service at Motumotu was greatly disturbed by the troublesome antics of a young man. At the close, Chalmers took the youth by the hand in order to hold him while talking with him about his behavior. This was resented by the young man and his friends. The church was quickly surrounded by a crowd of excited, armed men. Their leader was brandishing a huge broad sword. Tamate sprang to the door, met the leader on the steps and dexterously wrenched the broad sword from his grasp. Seeing their leader thus disarmed, the mob dispersed.

The state of her health having become very serious, Mrs. Chalmers left for England in March, 1892, after a pathetic parting with her husband at Thursday Island. Greatheart then turned to a work he had long been hoping and praying to undertake, namely, the exploration of the Fly River district, with a view to the eventual establishment of mission stations along the course of this mighty river. He chose Saguane on Kiwai Island in the Fly River delta as his new base of operations and settled there a teacher named Maru and his wife. He looked upon this new enterprise as probably the most hazardous, the greatest and the last of his life. He wrote in his diary, "God knows there will be many Gethsemanes and it may be many Calvarys, but all for Christ and all is well." In January, 1893, the long awaited launch arrived and was named the *Miro*. He found this a great help but it soon became apparent that the swift current of the Fly River demanded a larger vessel with more powerful engines.

In March, 1894, he received a cablegram calling him to England to be one of the principal speakers in the centenary celebrations of the London Missionary Society. He was happy to see his wife again. Her health, however, was far from robust, so when he returned to New Guinea in January, 1896, he returned alone. For months he traveled in boats, often wet from morning till night, visiting the established stations and endeavoring to establish new ones. He was constantly sailing up new rivers, visiting new tribes, braving new perils. What was it that lured him on? He said, "I dearly love to be the first to preach Christ in a place."

All his life Chalmers had a passionate love for water. The romantic experiences of his youth were associated with lakes and other places containing water. Most of his missionary work was done as he traveled by water. He was exhilarated at the sight of water—up the stream, at the surf, on the sea. He often wondered, he states, "what sort of place heaven would be without sea, without water." And it was the supreme delight of his life to point thirsty souls to the fountain of the Water of Life and to repeat the divine entreaty: "Whosoever will, come, drink and live."

VI. IN THE TEXT HE HEARD THE STATELY CADENCES OF LOVE'S MIGHTY MONOSYLLABLE

The Papuans loved to hear Tamate sing. On numerous occasions it was his singing, accompanied perhaps by the Christian teachers that stilled the angry tumult in the breasts of murderous savages.

The song he often sang—the first song he translated and taught to the native Christians—was "Come to Jesus." It was the old, old text set to music! In Revelation 22:17 the word "Come" is found in the opening sentence and is then thrice reiterated. If every word in the Bible except one had to be blotted out, Chalmers would choose to cling to this mighty monosyllable—"COME!"

It was Revelation 22:17 set to music.
It was the music of the divine solicitude.
It was the music of love's mighty monosyllable.

As Tamate traveled about, he experienced many inconveniences, not the least of which was that resulting from the native practice of rubbing noses by way of greeting and of expressing friendly sentiments. The inconveniences arose partly from the vigor and the frequency with which the practice was indulged and partly from the fact that the faces of the natives were commonly coated with filthy pigments of various colors. Concerning one such experience Tamate once said: "About one hundred and fifty natives are around us shouting, yelling and rubbing noses. Alas, alas, I cannot say I like this nose-rubbing. Having no looking glass I cannot tell the state of my face but I know that my nose is flattened out and my face one mass of pigment."

Chalmers lived to see the first fruits of harvest. He was privileged to baptize hundreds of earnest converts and to see other hundreds under Christian instruction, meeting on the Lord's Day in the chapels built by native hands. In August, 1897, Mrs. Chalmers returned to New Guinea and entered with joy into the work. A letter written by her in January, 1900, shows what progress had been made at Saguane. About seventeen hundred people attended the New Year services. Three hundred participated in a solemn communion service and one hundred and thirty-six adults were baptized. It was marvelous to see people of different tribes assembling in friendly fashion, who a few years before were almost constantly engaged in sanguinary conflicts. Mrs. Chalmers became critically ill in the summer of that year and died at Daru October 26. She left a legacy with which to procure an excellent new whaleboat for her husband's use in opening up the Fly River area for Christ.

To this work he turned, haunted by a vision of teeming multitudes of Papuans who knew nothing of the Saviour. Robert Louis Stevenson wrote a friend: "Tamate is away now to go up the Fly River, a desperate venture, it is thought. He is quite a Livingstone card." In a letter to his mother the great writer said, "I hope I shall meet Tamate once more before he disappears up the Fly River, perhaps to be one of 'the unreturning brave.'" The words proved prophetic, for a little later he went out to return no more.

In April, 1901 Chalmers set out to visit the district around Cape Blackwood, on the eastern side of the Fly River delta. He knew this area was inhabited by a particularly ferocious tribe of savages who were both skull-hunters and cannibals. He was accompanied by Rev. Oliver Tomkins, a promising young colleague recently arrived from England. At a place called Risk Point on the island of Goaribari a swarm of natives, with all sorts of weapons, came in canoes and took forcible possession of the mission vessel as it lay anchored off shore. Tamate decided to go ashore, but, anticipating trouble, urged Mr. Tomkins to remain aboard the vessel. Mr. Tomkins, however, insisted on sharing whatever dangers might await his beloved leader, so the two went ashore together to the village of Dopina. This was on April 8, 1901. Those on board the vessel never saw them again.

A few days later the Christian world was stunned by a cablegram stating that James Chalmers and his young colleague had been killed and eaten by the Fly River cannibals.

It was ascertained later that, when Chalmers, Tomkins and several boys from the mission school got ashore, they were invited into the dubu of the village to have something to eat. As soon as they entered, the signal was given for a general massacre. The two missionaries were hit on the head from behind with stone clubs and fell senseless to the floor. Their heads were immediately cut off, then their followers were similarly killed and beheaded. The heads were distributed as trophies among the murderers, while the bodies were handed over to the women to cook. The flesh was mixed with sago and was eaten the same day by the wildly exulting cannibals.

Yes, it was reported that James Chalmers, the Greatheart of New Guinea, was dead, but John Oxenham thought otherwise.

> *Greatheart is dead, they say!*
> *Not dead, nor sleeping! He lives on! His name*
> *Shall kindle many a heart to equal flame;*
> *The fire he kindled shall burn on and on*
> *Till all the darkness of the lands be gone,*
> *And all the kingdoms of the earth be won.*
> *A soul so fiery sweet can never die,*
> *But lives and loves and works through all eternity.*

And so it was that Greatheart was called to a higher realm of service. He now heard the same, sweet voice he heard at Inverary long ago and the invitation was the same—"Come!" Having made the abodes of cannibalism echo the sweet accents of the Great Invitation, he now turned his face toward the city foursquare; and as his last climbing footstep took him across the threshold of the Celestial City, he heard once again the stately cadences of love's mighty monosyllable.

JAMES CHALMERS

QUESTIONS, TOPICS, AND ASSIGNMENTS
FOR STUDY

1. What was Chalmers's life text? Is there any special reason why this verse became his text?

2. Note the facts of Chalmers's first seventeen years of life. In his love for the sea, what qualities did he exhibit that helped to fit him for his missionary work in New Guinea?

3. Describe Chalmers's conversion experience. What did he later say concerning this experience?

4. What part of this life text urged Chalmers to repeat the Gospel message to others? How did he begin to do this?

5. What constituted Chalmers's call? What was his missionary preparation?

6. Under what missionary society did Chalmers and his wife go out? Briefly relate their experiences on board ship.

7. What four main methods did Chalmers use on the island of Rarotonga in order to direct sinners to "the Lamb of God"?

8. Why was Chalmers dissatisfied with his work at Rarotonga?

9. Describe the people, the customs and the land of New Guinea. Why did the natives think Tamate had come to their country?

10. For a brief clear account of magic see C.H. Smith—*The Missionary and Primitive Man*, pp. 137-141.

11. Describe Tamate's unique methods of making friends with savages.

12. What was one of Tamate's narrow escapes with savages?

13. What was Mrs. Chalmers's attitude toward the mission work? Note the facts of her last days on earth.

14. Describe the rainmaker's conversion and death.

15. What was Chalmers's relationship with Robert Louis Stevenson? Why did Stevenson wish he had met Tamate when he was a youth?

16. Note the experiences of Tamate and the native teacher at Mailu.

17. What was the incident of Tamate and his two friends among the cannibals of the Orokolo and Maipua districts?

18. What is anthropophagy? What are the three chief reasons for cannibalism? Gordon Smith—*The Missionary and Primitive Man* pp. 189, 190.

19. Describe the atrocity and ensuing tension at Kalo, Thought for Christians—what would happen if one tenth of the professing Christians in America had the kind of zeal that Chalmers and his humble native helpers had?

20. How long was Chalmers's first term on the mission field? What was his attitude toward these years of service? What three important things happened while he was back in his homeland?

21. Can you detect the motive in "nose eating"?

22. Where were his new headquarters? Describe the conditions there.

23. What was the disposition of Tamate's second wife? How did she help her husband in the mission work?

24. Describe the boat trip to Moveave.

25. How did Chalmers seek an improvement of his wife's health?

26. What did Tamate consider his most hazardous enterprise? What enabled him to begin this exploration?

27. Why did Greatheart once again go to England in 1894? On his return what was the nature of his work?

28. Did Chalmers see the fruit of his missionary labor? How?

29. What was done with the money which Mrs. Chalmers left at her death?

30. What was Chalmers's last area of service? By whom was he accompanied?

31. At what place did the final catastrophe take place? What was this catastrophe? When did it happen? What was the report concerning it?

32. To what was Greatheart finally called?

33. What is the status of missionary work in New Guinea today?

ADDITIONAL BIOGRAPHIES ON CHALMERS

James Chalmers—*Pioneering in New Guinea.*

Richard Lovett—*Tamate*: *The Life and Story of James Chalmers.*

JONATHAN GOFORTH

THE HOLY SPIRIT'S MAN IN CHINA
(1859 – 1936)

At a Summer conference meeting near Chicago it was announced that a "brilliant speaker" was to be present on a certain day for just one address. At the appointed time the chairman introduced the speaker with an extravagant eulogy, whereupon the speaker stepped forward, stood a few moments in silent prayer, then said:

> *Friends, if you and I take glory to ourselves which belongs only to God, we are as foolish as the woodpecker about which I shall tell you. A certain woodpecker flew up to the top of a high pine tree and gave three hard pecks on the side of the tree as woodpeckers are wont to do. At that instant a bolt of lightning struck the tree, leaving it on the ground, a heap of splinters. The woodpecker had flown to a tree nearby where it clung in terror and amazement at what had taken place. There it hung expecting more to follow, but as all remained quiet it began to chuckle to itself saying, "Well, well, well. Who would have imagined that just three pecks of my beak could have such power as that!"*

That was one of Jonathan Goforth's favorite stories and with good reason. Few Christians have been so tempted to carnal pride as was he, for few have been the human instrument of such remarkable revivals or the object of such praise. A Roman Catholic servant girl, in a home where the Goforth's often visited, said, "I have often watched Dr. Goforth's face and wondered if God looks like him." Charles G. Trumbull said of him, "He was an electric, radiant personality, flooding his immediate environment with sunlight that was deep in his heart and shone on his face. And God used him in mighty revivals." It was as true of Goforth as of Robert M. M'Cheyne that all who knew him "felt the breathing of the hidden life of God." He knew the folly of self-reliance. He knew whence power came and to whom the praise belonged. So as a young man he chose Zechariah 4:6 as his life's motto.

> *The sunlight in his heart!*
> *The divine reflection on his face!*
> *The breathing of the hidden life of God!*
> *Not by might nor by power but by my spirit, saith the Lord.*

Everything in the character and career of this amazing man can be outlined in terms of the work and witness of the Holy Spirit in his yielded, trusting life.

I. BY THE SPIRIT GOFORTH FOUND THE SAVIOR AND DEVOTED HIMSELF TO HIS SERVICE

Jonathan Goforth, the seventh of eleven children, was born February 10, 1859, on his father's farm near London, Ontario, Canada. His devout mother influenced him to pray, love, read and memorize the Scriptures. Something of the hardships endured by the family is indicated by the fact that the father once went to Hamilton for food and walked seventy miles back through the bush with a sack of flour on his back. By diligent effort Jonathan managed to keep up with his class in school although he was under the handicap of being obliged to work on the farm each year from April to October.

At fifteen his father put him in charge of their second farm twenty miles from the home farm. "Work hard" said his father. "At harvest I'll return and inspect." In later years Goforth stirred many an audience with the re-telling of his arduous labors that summer, of his father's return in the fall and of how his heart thrilled when his father, after inspecting the fields of beautiful waving grain, turned to him and smiled. "That smile," he would say, "was all the reward I wanted. I knew my father was pleased. So will it be, dear Christians, if we are faithful to the trust our Heavenly Father has given us. His smile of approval will be our blessed reward."

At eighteen, while finishing his high school work, Jonathan came under the influence of Rev. Lachlan Cameron, a true minister of Christ. He had attended Rev. Cameron's church one Sunday where he heard a sermon from God's Word that cut deeply and suited his need exactly. The Holy Spirit used the Word to bring him under conviction, and that day he yielded to the tender constraints of Christ. "Henceforth," said he, "my life belongs to Him who gave His life for me."

Under this impulse Jonathan became an active, growing Christian. He sent for a supply of tracts and startled the staid Presbyterian elders by standing, Sunday after Sunday, at the church door handing them out to all who entered. Soon thereafter he began a Sunday evening service in an old schoolhouse about a mile from his home. He instituted the practice of family worship and besought the Lord for the salvation of his father. Several months later his father took a public stand for Christ.

About this time Jonathan's faith was subjected to a severe testing. His teacher was a blatant follower of the infidel, Tom Paine, and his classmates, influenced by the teacher, made Jonathan's life miserable by their jeers and mockery. The foundations seemed to be giving way and in a mood of desperation, he turned to God's Word. In consequence of an earnest, day-and-night search of the Word, his faith was firmly established and all his classmates, including his teacher, were brought back from infidelity. The next great influence in Jonathan's life came through a book and later, a collection of books.

A saintly old Scotchman, Mr. Bennett, one day handed him a well-worn copy of the Memoirs of Robert Murray M'Cheyne, saying, "Read this, my boy; it will do you good." It did! Stretched out on the dry leaves in the woods, he became so absorbed in the book that he failed to notice the passing hours. When the lengthening shadows of sunset aroused him, he arose a new man. The story of M'Cheyne's spiritual struggles, sacrifices and victories stirred him to the depths and was used of God's Spirit to turn his life away from selfish ambitions to, instead, the holy calling of being a seeker of souls. In view of his intention to enter Knox College to prepare for the ministry, Rev. Cameron arranged to give him lessons in Latin and Greek and loaned him a number of books by Bunyan, Baxter, Boston and Spurgeon, which he "devoured" with rich blessing. But his main book was the Bible. He arose two hours earlier each morning in order to have unhurried time for the study of the Word before going to work or to school.

Young Goforth was now spiritually ready for God to deal with him again. One epochal day he went to hear an address by the heroic missionary pioneer, George L. Mackay of Formosa. Full of the Holy Spirit, like Peter and Paul and Stephen of old, Dr. Mackay pressed home the needs and claims of the heathen world, especially that of Formosa. He told how he had been seeking missionary reinforcements far and wide in Canada but, so far, had not found one young man willing to respond. Simply but powerfully, he continued, "I am going back alone. It will not be long before my bones will be lying on some Formosan hillside. To me the heartbreak is that no young man has heard the call to come and carry on the work that I have begun."

As Goforth heard these words he was "overwhelmed with shame." He describes his reactions as follows: "There was I, bought with the precious blood of Jesus Christ, daring to dispose of my life as I pleased. Then and there I capitulated to Christ. From that hour I became a foreign missionary."

Note well the words, "From that hour I became a foreign missionary." An ocean voyage does not transform a lukewarm Christian into a glowing brand for God.

II. BY THE SPIRIT GOFORTH WAS A BLAZING BRAND FOR GOD IN TORONTO

Jonathan's mother was a capable seamstress, and in the last days before his departure for Knox College often worked far into the night preparing his wardrobe. Little did she imagine how the cut of his garments and the fine hand stitches would cause him to be an object of ridicule in the city. He arrived at the college with ardent expectations concerning the friendly reception and Christian fellowship that awaited him. However, he was soon disillusioned by the students' glances and guffaws. Despite his very limited finances, he determined to alter the situation by purchasing a quantity of cloth so a city seamstress could tailor him a new outfit. Learning what he had done, his college mates took him from his room by force one night, put his head through a hole cut in one end of the material, and made him drag the cloth up and down the hall through a gauntlet of hilarious students. In his humiliation that such a thing could happen in a Christian college, he spent hours over his Bible and on his knees in the first great struggle of his life.

During his first day in Toronto, Jonathan walked through the slums praying that God would open a way whereby he might take the Gospel to Toronto's needy homes and needy hearts. Each Sunday morning found him preaching in a jail, and he continued to do so throughout his college career. As unreservedly as his studies would allow, he gave himself to evangelistic calling in the homes of the slums and to the work of different rescue missions. The stories he told of his experiences with degraded sinners caused much mirth among the students. It is significant, however, that later the students of Knox College sent him to China as their missionary —a remarkable tribute to the reality and power of his Christian character.

Jonathan exhibited a fervent zeal for souls. At the opening of a new fall session at college, the principal asked him how many homes he had visited during the summer vacation. "Nine hundred sixty," was the reply. "Well, Goforth, if you don't take any scholarships in Greek and Hebrew, at least there is one book that you are going to be well versed in and that is the book of Canadian human nature." Indeed, not only were many souls saved but many valuable lessons learned, for, as he would discover later, there is no essential difference between Canadian and Chinese human nature. During his college years and while working in the slums, he was often down to the last penny. But God proved faithful in every test. Like George Muller and Hudson Taylor, Jonathan learned to trust God utterly for all his needs.

Jonathan also learned to trust the Spirit's guidance in all circumstances. On one occasion, for example, when scheduled to speak at a certain place on Sunday, he found he had only enough money to purchase a ticket one station short of where he was to speak. After praying for divine guidance, he bought his ticket and rode to that station then began to walk the remaining ten miles. Eight miles later he came upon a group of men repairing the road. He engaged them in friendly conversation, pointed them to "the only name given under Heaven whereby we must be saved" and invited them to the service the following day. To his great joy several of them turned up and at least one of them was saved. Later referring to this, he would say, "I would gladly walk ten miles any day to bring one lost soul to Christ." He was indeed a missionary long before he reached China. It was said of him, "When he found his own soul needed Jesus Christ, it became a passion with him to take Jesus Christ to every soul."

Not hesitating to enter saloons and brothels, Jonathan Goforth won for Christ a number of broken, disreputable persons. One night, coming out of a street that had a particularly evil reputation, a policeman met Goforth and said, "How have you the courage to go into those places? We policemen never go there except in twos or threes."

"I never walk alone either," replied Goforth. "There is always Someone with me."

Another time he called at every house along the ten mile road from Aspidin to Huntsville. Years later a lady wrote of the abiding blessings that ensued upon the visits of this "Spirit-filled young man" concluding how, "He walked in the power of the Holy Spirit."

"I never walk alone!"
"I would walk ten miles any day to bring one soul to Christ!"
"He walked in the power of the Holy Spirit!"

It was in connection with his mission work in Toronto that Goforth met an Episcopalian, Rosalind Bell-Smith. A member of a cultured and wealthy family and an artist, Rosalind was also a born-again Christian and longed to live a life of service to God. The day she met Goforth she noted both the shabbiness of his dress and the challenge of his eyes. A few days later at a mission meeting she picked up Jonathan's Bible, which was lying on a chair, observed that it was marked from cover to cover, and noted how parts of it were almost in shreds from frequent use. "That's the man I want to marry" she said to herself. A few months later she accepted his proposal of marriage upon the condition he himself stipulated, namely, that in all things he should put his Master's work before her. Little did she dream what that promise would cost her through the long years ahead. The first, though not the greatest price it cost her, was the engagement ring of which she had dreamed. For Jonathan explained that he needed every penny for his ministry of distributing Testaments and tracts. "This," she said, "was my first lesson in real values."

In the spring of 1887 Goforth went to scores of churches to plead the cause of China. He was on fire for missions and his holy enthusiasm melted thousands of indifferent hearts. When he was speaking on the needs and claims of the unevangelized worlds he had the face of an angel and the tongue of an archangel. He used many methods— Scripture, charts, pictures, logic – to enforce his message. He often closed an address by a powerful illustration from the feeding of the five thousand. He pictured the disciples taking the bread and fish to the hungry people on the first few rows, then going again and again to those same people, leaving those on the back rows hungry and starving. Then he would ask a burning question. "What would Christ have thought of His disciples had they acted in that way, and what does He think of us today as we continue to spend most of our time and money in giving the Bread of Life to those who have heard so often, while hundreds of millions in China are still starving?"

Years later when Goforth was home on furlough and speaking in a Vancouver, Presbyterian church, the minister who introduced him said, "This man took an overcoat from me once." He went on to explain how he had gone to Toronto to buy a new overcoat and how, at a missionary meeting, was stirred as never before upon listening to the impassioned appeal of Jonathan Goforth. "My precious overcoat money went into the missionary collection," continued the minister, "and I returned home wearing my old coat."

October 25, 1887, Jonathan and Rosalind were married. After a memorable farewell service in Toronto's historic Knox Church, the

Goforths sailed for China on February 4, 1888, under the auspices of the Canadian Presbyterian Church.

III. BY THE SPIRIT GOFORTH PIONEERED AS AN EVANGELIST AND CHURCH PLANTER IN CHINA

The Goforths settled first at Chefoo for nine months of language study. While living there some valuable lessons were learned. About two weeks after settling in Chefoo, their house burned to the ground and practically everything they owned was destroyed. Mrs. Goforth was distraught, but her husband simply said, "My dear, do not grieve so. After all, they're just things." Thus Rosalind learned another lesson in real values. It was also at Chefoo she learned a lesson in tithing. She had considered themselves generous in tithing their missionary salary. But when they had been married six months it was discovered they had already given a tenth of a year's salary. "We'll simply close the account and keep on tithing," Jonathan said. So they gave two tithes instead of one.

With elation of spirit the Goforths moved further and further into the interior on the way to the remote province of Honan to set up a home and a mission station. Their early years in China were marked by sweet joys, piercing sorrows and significant manifestations of character. The chief sorrows were connected with the untimely passing of their first two children. Their severe heartache was swallowed up in their travail over the woes of the Chinese masses. The word without was written in giant letters over the blackness of heathenism on every side as the Goforths moved along.

Men and women were toiling without a Bible, without a Sunday, without prayer, without songs of praise. They had homes without peace, marriage without sanctity, little children without innocence, young men and girls without ideals, poverty without relief or sympathy, sickness without skillful help or tender care, sorrow and crime without a remedy, and death without hope.

Before reaching Honan, Goforth had received a cordial letter from Hudson Taylor telling of the tremendous obstacles ahead and reminding him of his need of supernatural assistance. "Brother, if you would enter that province," Taylor wrote, "you must go forward on your knees." Goforth did just that. Not a day passed but that circumstances and events caused him to recall his life text and to rely on its promise, "Not by might nor by power but by my Spirit, saith the Lord."

By means of prayer and dependence upon the Holy Spirit, Jonathan Goforth witnessed and experienced many miracles, one of which was in connection with language study. In Knox College he was weak in languages and in China he made little progress in the use of the language, although he applied himself to the task with great diligence. Repeatedly, when he tried to preach to a group of people, the Chinese would point to another missionary who had reached China a year after he did to say, "You speak. We don't understand him." This was mortifying but Goforth refused to be discouraged. "The Lord called me to China," he said, "and I expect His Spirit to perform a miracle and to enable me to master the language." He picked up his Chinese Bible and went to the chapel. As he began to preach, the miracle happened; he spoke with a fluency and power that amazed the people and thenceforth his mastery of the Chinese language was recognized everywhere. Two months later he received a letter from Knox College telling of a prayer meeting in which the students prayed "just for Goforth" and the presence of God was manifestly among them. Looking into his diary he found that the prayer meeting was held at the very time his tongue gained such sudden mastery over the Chinese language.

His zeal for souls caused him to be away from home much of the time in widespread evangelistic itineration. He often spent the night in places that were disagreeable for lack of heat and for other reasons. For instance: "One end of the small room I occupied was for the pigs and donkeys. Besides, we had to contend against other living things not so big as donkeys but a thousand times more troublesome." There were many escapes from wild mobs. One day he and a colleague came suddenly into a crowd of thousands attending a sort of fair. Though both foreigners wore Chinese dress, their identity was soon recognized and in a few moments the crowd rushed them, hooting, yelling, throwing sticks, stones and clods of earth. Just when death seemed imminent, a sudden gust of wind blew a tent over and scattered the articles offered for sale. As the Chinese scrambled for these, the missionaries escaped.

A common method of transportation was to ride in a hired wheelbarrow. Goforth soon found out, however, that if he rode, his Chinese helpers also insisted on riding although they had never before been accustomed or able to do so. To defeat this pride, he bought a barrow for four dollars and hired a man to wheel it for about fifteen cents a day. He wrote:

> *I shall not allow myself a ride on this barrow nor shall I allow a Chinese the luxury. I am determined to walk. The barrow conveys books and baggage, not missionaries. My expenditure, including the barrow man's hire, amounted to twenty-four cents a day for the thirty-three days of my tour.*

This intrepid missionary constantly lived up to his name, for he was ever eager to "go forth" to new areas and new conquests for Christ. In 1894 and 1895 he went to Changte, in remote North Hogan, bought land, erected buildings, established a mission station and moved the family belongings. This was, for the Goforths, the seventh home in their seven years in China. Even before settling in the seventh home the mission compound was covered by flood waters to a depth of more than six feet and thus, for the second time, they experienced the loss of practically all of their temporal possessions.

The air was filled with wild rumors about the foreign devils. One of these was to the effect that the medicine used by the foreigners in treating the people was made from the hearts and eyes of kidnapped Chinese children. But the Spirit of God was at work and such crowds waited upon the ministry of the Word that both Goforth and his wife "kept up constant preaching on an average of eight hours a day" and were at the point of complete physical exhaustion. Early one morning he said, "Rose, on the basis of Philippians 4:19 let us kneel down and pray for an evangelist to help us in the work." This they did though as yet they had not a single convert in this area. The next day a man named Wang Fulin appeared at the mission seeking employment. He was a pitiable spectacle, his face having the ashy hue of an opium fiend, his form bent from weakness and emaciated frame, clothed in a beggar's rags, shaking every few moments from a racking cough. This man became a mighty testimony to the transforming power of Christ and a fervent preacher of the Gospel. In the first five months at Changte about twenty-five thousand men and women visited the compound and heard the precious tidings of redemption proclaimed by the Goforths and the converted gambler and opium smoker, Wang Fulin.

With their new semiforeign bungalow completed, the Chinese came in swarms to see the board floors, glass windows, the furniture, the sewing machine and the organ. The kitchen stove, which sent its smoke up the chimney instead of into people's eyes and all over the house, was an object of constant wonder. The pump was the talk of the whole countryside. What a contraption that could bring water up from the bottom of a well without a bucket! As many as 1,835 men and 500 women passed through the house on a single day and all heard the Gospel message.

Rosalind frequently played the organ to the great delight of the Chinese. Jonathan, however, did not know one note from another. Imagine her surprise and amusement when, upon returning from an errand one day, she found her husband seated at the organ with all twenty-four stops drawn out, his hands pressed down on as many notes as possible, the bellows going at full blast, and heard someone remark above the din, "He plays better than his wife!"

By this time they had three living children to rejoice their hearts. Then, in the summer of 1898, little Gracie was found to be in a hopeless condition from an enlarged spleen caused by pernicious malaria; she lingered and suffered for almost a year. One night Gracie sat up in bed and said, "I want my Papa." Rosalind hesitated to call the worn-out father but when Gracie said again, "I want my Papa," she roused him. As the father took the little one in his arms and began to pace the floor, Rosalind went into another room and prayed that God would heal the dear child or spare her from further suffering. While the mother was on her knees, Gracie suddenly lifted her head from her father's shoulder, looked straight into his eyes, gave him a wonderful smile, and closed her eyes. In an instant she was in the Savior's arms.

Goforth was singularly adept at devising ways of meeting difficult situations and appealing to various types of people. At a certain time each year thousands of students came to Changte to take examinations for government positions. Large numbers of them came to the mission but were full of conceit, disorderly, and impossible to control. Planning to be ready for them the next year, he sent to Shanghai for a large globe, several maps and astronomical charts. When groups of students came they immediately asked, "What is that big round thing?" He would explain that it was a representation of the earth. "You don't mean to tell us that the earth is round, do you?" they would reply in astonishment. When he explained the movements of the earth some were sure to exclaim, "If the earth turns like that, why don't we all tumble off?" Then followed explanations concerning the law of gravitation, the size of the sun, its distance from the earth and other astronomical facts. Thus pride was dispelled and hundreds of students listened attentively to the story of Christ and redeeming love.

The missionary had a passion for preaching, a longing to develop the converts into New Testament Christians and a zeal to establish spiritual, indigenous, New Testament churches after the Pauline pattern. Taking a group of native Christians with him he would "go from town to town and from street to street preaching and singing the Gospel in true Salvation Army style." A map of the field was made and each center where a Christian church or group had come into existence was indicated by a red dot. By May of 1900 there were over fifty of these red dots. Both parents and children delighted to watch the dots increase. Florence, the oldest daughter, aged 7, exclaimed one day, "Oh won't it be lovely, father, when the map is all red?" The work of God was progressing mightily. "Our hearts are aglow with the victories of the present and the promises of the future," wrote Goforth. And for the hundredth or thousandth time he quoted his great text, "We expect a great harvest of souls, for it is not by the might or power of man but by my Spirit, saith the Lord."

> *The victories of the present!*
> *The promised of the future!*
> *A great harvest of souls!*
> *It is by my Spirit, saith the Lord!*

IV. BY THE SPIRIT GOFORTH WAS ENDUED WITH POWER FROM ON HIGH AND PROMOTED MIGHTY REVIVALS

During the early months of 1900 the hearts of the missionaries were radiant with blessing and hope. Then came the storm. In June golden-haired Florence was smitten with meningitis and "went to be with Jesus." The funeral was scarcely over when a message came from the American Consul in Chefoo saying, "Flee south. Northern route cut off Boxers." The terrors and horrors of the infamous Boxer Uprising were descending. The missionaries were in favor of staying at their post regardless of the consequences, but the Chinese Christians made it clear that their chances of escape would be greatly reduced if the missionaries remained. On June 28, before daybreak, the missionary party, consisting of the Goforths and their four children, plus three men, five women and one little boy, set out on the long and hazardous journey fourteen days by cart to Fancheng and a longer period from there by boat to Shanghai. These were days of panic and agony due to the intense heat, the long hours of continual bumping over rough roads in springless carts, the illness of one of the children and the oft repeated cries, "Kill these foreign devils" that came from fierce, threatening mobs along the way.

At one point a mob of several hundred men attacked them with a fusillade of stones. As Goforth ruched forward to reason with the men, he was struck on the head and body by numerous savage blows and one arm was slashed to the bone in several places. Dripping with blood, he staggered to the cart, picked up his baby and said, "Come! We must get away quickly." Rosalind and other missionaries received very painful injuries, but all managed to escape as the mob scrambled for their possessions in the carts.

After many terrifying experiences and narrow escapes they reached Shanghai and soon sailed for Canada. The furlough was a time of poignant sorrow as Goforth, in his deputation trips, found that worldliness and apostasy had invaded the churches and most of the people had little concern for the unsaved masses of heathen lands.

Back to China they went; to the people they loved, to the multitudes they yearned to win for Christ, to the land where all their possessions had been destroyed four times and where four of their children were buried. Jonathan was soon enthusiastic over a plan of intensive evangelism which would entail their staying in successive centers for a period of one month each. "I will go with my men," he said to Rosalind, "to villages or on the streets in the day time, while you receive and preach to the women in the courtyard." The evenings would be devoted to open air meetings.

At the end of a month an evangelist would be left to instruct the converts and establish a congregation. "The plan sounds wonderful," replied Rosalind, "except for the children. Think of all the infectious diseases and of our four little graves. I can't do it. I cannot expose the children like that." He, however, was sure of God's leading in the matter and said, "Rose, I fear for the children if you refuse to obey God's call and stay here at Changte. The safest place for you and the children is the path of duty." A few hours later Wallace became seriously ill with Asiatic dysentery. After two weeks he began to recover and Jonathan packed up and set out on tour alone. The next day the baby, Constance, fell ill and the father was sent for. Constance was dying when he arrived. Driven by sorrow, Rosalind leaned her head upon the Heavenly Father's bosom and prayed, "O God, it is too late for Constance but I will trust you hereafter for everything, including my children."

Thenceforth, for years, she and the children traveled almost constantly with Goforth in his extensive evangelistic tours. This meant that some things loved and prized by the family had to be given up, such as flowers, bird, dog and cat. It also meant living simply, in native Chinese style. Usually the furnishings of the rented native house consisted of a table, two chairs, a bench for the children and a *kang*—a long brick platform bed covered with loose straw and straw mats where the entire family slept if the vermin, insects and pigs permitted them to do so!

Goforth's evangelistic methods were simple and spiritual. Whether speaking to one person or a thousand, he was never known to attempt to deal with souls without his open Bible. His love for and dependence upon the Word is indicated by the fact that he read through and studied his Chinese New Testament fifty-five times during a period of nineteen years. He also used large hymn scrolls as a means of utilizing the people's love of singing and of teaching the Gospel's great truths, in addition to short Gospel messages and testimonies. They lived as a family for one month in every place and carried on this type of intensive evangelistic effort until a growing church was subsequently established.

At the age of forty-four a strange restlessness came over Jonathan Goforth. He had seen hundreds of precious souls saved and scores of churches established. But his soul burned with an indescribable longing to enter into the fulfillment of his Lord's promise, "Verily, verily, I say unto you, he that believeth on me, the works that I do shall he do also and greater works than these shall he do." Tidings of the mighty revival in Wales intensified this longing, as did also a booklet containing selections from Finney's *Lectures on Revival.* Again and again he read Kinney's argument that the spiritual laws governing a spiritual harvest are as real and dependable as the laws of agriculture and natural harvest. At length he said, "If Kinney is right, and I believe his is, I am going to find out what these spiritual laws are and obey them, no matter what the cost may be." He began an intense study of every passage in the Bible dealing with the Holy Spirit. He arose regularly at five o'clock or even earlier for Bible study and to pray for the fullness of the Spirit. One evening while speaking to an audience of unsaved people on "He bore our sins in His own body on the tree," he saw deep conviction written on every face and almost every one took an open stand for Christ. Shortly thereafter he visited Korea and was stirred by participation in remarkable outpourings of revival power.

In 1908 he accepted invitations to conduct revival efforts in Manchuria. He did not deal in pious battery. He told of the amazing results in Korea—of dynamic New Testament Christianity, of the quality and astounding increase of converts, of schools and churches, all self-supporting—and pointed out the humiliating contrast in the paucity of spiritual results in Manchuria. Wherein lay the difference? It could not be accounted for on grounds of war and political unrest in Manchuria, for Korea had had her full share of these. The marvelous results in Korea, he emphasized, were "not by might nor by power but by my spirit, saith the Lord."

The difference was in the degree of yieldedness to the Spirit and of readiness to pay the price of spiritual power. Goforth himself had paid that price—in prayer and in penitence. A spirit of estrangement had arisen between him and a fellow missionary. When he tried to preach, the Lord spoke to him, "You hypocrite. You know you do not really love your brother. If you do not straighten this thing out, I cannot bless you." Realizing that he was just beating the air, he yielded and said, "Lord, just as soon as this meeting is over I'll go and set this matter straight." Instantly God's power surged upon him and his preaching was "in the demonstration of the Spirit." Upon the meeting being thrown open for prayer, many arose to pray only to break down weeping. "For almost twenty years," said Goforth, "we missionaries in Hogan had longed in vain to see a tear of penitence roll down a Chinese cheek." He did effect a full reconciliation with his fellow missionary and thenceforth the Spirit could use the yielded, cleansed life.

Those were days of unprecedented spiritual awakening. As a result, he was deluged with invitations from all parts of China and found himself drawn into a new and far-reaching type of ministry. Rosalind and the five children sailed for Canada and he, a lonely man separated from his family till his next furlough time, plunged into the greatest work of his life.

One day at the close of his message he said to the people, "You may pray." Immediately an elder of the church, with tears streaming down his cheeks, stood before the congregation and confessed the sins of theft, adultery and attempted murder. "I have disgraced the holy office," he cried. "I herewith resign my eldership." Other elders, then the deacons, arose one by one, confessed their sins and resigned. Then the native pastor stood up, made his confession and concluded, "I am not fit to be your pastor any longer, I, too, must resign." As the Christians confessed their sins and got right with God, large numbers of unbelievers came under deep conviction and were saved. Some of the missionaries were entirely out of sympathy with these revivals. One man said, "Don't expect any such praying and confessing of sins here as took place in Mukden and Liaoyang. We're hard headed Presbyterians from the North of Ireland and the people take after us. Anyhow, we have respectable people here, not terrible sinners. Be prepared for a quiet Quakers' meeting at this place." But several days later the Pastor and many others sobbed out their confession. The whole congregation did the unheard of thing of getting down on their knees in prayer, and there was a mighty turning to God in that place.

Many times there was so much praying and confessing, little or no time was left for the message; even so, the meetings often lasted for three, four or even six hours. At Kwangchow, God's Spirit worked mightily, the church was cleansed and edified, one hundred fifty-four converts were baptized during the eight day meeting and the number of Christians in the city increased in four years from 2,000 to 8,000. At Shangtehfu there was an intense desire on the part of missionaries and Chinese Christians alike for a blessing from Heaven. Long before daylight the pleadings of earnest hearts arose to the Throne of Grace. One missionary sobbed out this prayer, "Lord, I have come to the place where I would rather pray than eat." In this place five hundred people openly acknowledged Christ as Savior. In a mission school where at first there was much antagonism, scores of boys were brought under the conviction of the Spirit. They confessed their sins, accepted Christ and brought a huge pile of pipes, cigarettes and tobacco to be destroyed and stolen knives and other things to be returned to their rightful owners.

Dr. Walter Philips, who at first was prejudiced against the revival movement, wrote of the meetings at Chinchow:

> *Now I understand why the floor was so wet—it was wet with pools of tears. Above the sobbing of hundreds of kneeling penitents, an agonized voice was making public confession. Others followed. The sight of men*

forced to their feet and impelled to lay bare their hearts brought the smarting tears to one's own eyes. And then again would swell the wonderful deep organ tone of united prayer, while men and women, lost to their surroundings, wrestled for peace.

Dr. P. C. Leslie said, "It was touching to see the distress of these pillars of the church, weeping in the presence of men because they had been humbled in the presence of God." Like the disciples at Pentecost, they were filled with the divine fullness and anointed with the Spirit's power.

Weeping in the presence of men!
Humbled in the presence of God!
Filled with the divine fullness!
Anointed with the Spirit's power!

V. BY THE SPIRIT GOFORTH ENDURED MANIFOLD TRIALS AND ENTERED UPON HIS CORONATION

One of the songs Jonathan loved was this:

Lord, Crucified, give me a heart like Thine;
Teach me to love the dying souls around,
Oh, keep my heart in closest touch with Thee;
And give me love, pure Calvary love,
To bring the lost to Thee.

Those who, like Paul, have as their one sublime obsession, the bringing of lost souls to Christ, are sure to endure many trials. It was so of Goforth. His trials included severe attacks of various diseases, intense suffering from chronic carbuncles, beatings at the hands of Chinese mobs, long periods of separation from his family and the burial of five of his children in China. Another sore trial arose in connection with his furlough visits to the homeland as he came to realize the appalling inroads of modernism and worldliness among the churches and the consequent apathy, even hostility, to his pleadings for missionary advance and a deeper work of the Spirit of God.

Speaking at the ministerial association, he told of the Spirit's quickening, purifying, energizing work in a certain city in China. He made it clear that he was no special favorite of the Almighty, that the same God was ready to pour out His Spirit in blessed revivals in Canada and that it was the business of every minister to look to the Holy Spirit for revival in his own heart and among his people. He went on to point out that John Wesley and his colleagues were just ordinary men until their hearts were touched by the divine fire. At that point a noted Methodist minister interrupted him. "What, sir!" he exclaimed, "Do you mean to tell me that we don't preach better now than John Wesley ever did?"

"Are you getting John Wesley's results?" Goforth asked.

The furlough of 1924 was spent chiefly in extended tours through the United States where he was enthusiastically received. His last years on the field were years of great harvest. Thousands were born into the kingdom and other thousands experienced the peace and power of the Spirit as he traveled extensively in China and Manchuria. On a single day he baptized 960 soldiers. A number of thriving churches were established. All of this was accomplished in spite of many hardships and much pain. During the 1930-1931 furlough, he lost the use of one eye and underwent many painful and fruitless operations in an attempt to restore his sight. During this time of illness, he dictated the stirring stories found in *Miracle Lives of China*. All his teeth had to be extracted and he contracted a severe infection in his jaw. It was at this time, while pacing the floor and holding his jaw with his hands, that he dictated the material for his famous book, *By My Spirit*. In China he contracted a severe case of pneumonia while preaching to a packed audience of sneezing, coughing people in an unheated room in the dead of winter. In 1933 he lost the sight of the other eye. Even during winter blizzards he continued traveling and preaching. At Taonan he was led two or three times daily through the deep snow and the storm to his appointments. A year later the Goforths returned to Canada because of a breakdown in Rosalind's health. Despite his blindness, he traveled widely in Canada and the United States. Everywhere he went his soul was aglow with one message, "the fullness of the Christ-life through the Holy Spirit's indwelling." Physical sight was gone, but his life was as "a dawning light that shineth more and more unto the perfect day."

That blessed day dawned for him in the early morning of October 8, 1936, as he slept. Just a few weeks before at the Ben Lippen conference in North Carolina, the sightless veteran missionary said he rejoiced in the thought that the next face he would see would be that of his Savior. He had entered into the bliss he had long anticipated: "I shall be satisfied when I awake with thy likeness" (Pa. 17:15). That was indeed his "coronation day" as Dr. Armstrong said at the funeral service in Knox Church, Toronto. In the words of Dr. Inkster, "Goforth was baptized with the Holy Ghost and with fire. He was filled with the Spirit because he was emptied of self."

> *The bliss he had long anticipated!*
> *The Saviour's face! The Saviour's likeness!*
> *Filled with the Spirit!*
> *Emptied of self!*
> *His Coronation Day!*

Jonathan Goforth's epitaph, written by the fingers of angels in letters of flaming lights, stands as a summons from heaven to all who read:

"NOT BY MIGHT NOR BY POWER, BUT BY MY SPIRIT, SAITH THE LORD."

JONATHAN GOFORTH

QUESTIONS, TOPICS, AND ASSIGNMENTS
FOR STUDY

1. What was Goforth's attitude toward pride? Cite Scripture references to indicate the Biblical viewpoint.

2. What was Goforth's great life text? In what ways did it characterize his activity?

      A.   As a young person?
      B.   As a student?
      C.   As a missionary?

3. Note the individuals whom God brought into Goforth's life and enriched the missionary's ministry.

4. What was Goforth's environment like as a child and as a student?

5. Explain the connotation of Mrs. Goforth's expression, "real values."

6. What was Goforth's frequent illustration to arouse zeal for foreign missions among his hearers?

7. What constituted his missionary call? What is your definition of a missionary call?

8. Did Goforth's missionary call influence his personal living? When? How?

9. What word well expresses the product of heathenism?

10. State the great aim of Goforth's life.

11. Compose a list of missionary qualifications as successfully demonstrated in Goforth's life and activity.

12. Make a chart on the basis of the five areas of Goforth's service as indicated by the author. State briefly the main incidents in each area.

13. How did Goforth conduct his deputation work as a candidate and as a missionary on furlough? Do you see in this some practical lessons for missionaries today?

14. Under what board were the Goforths appointed? Select a mission board in which you are interested. Report on the historical background, financial policies and candidate qualifications of this board.

15. Did Goforth learn the language easily? Discuss the importance and methods of language study today.

16. Did Goforth recognize the importance of establishing indigenous churches? What was the apostle Paul's attitude and practice in this matter?

17. What circumstances and means were used by the Holy Spirit in preparing Goforth for the Korean revival?
J. Goforth—*By My Spirit*, p. 228

18. Why was the Korean revival called "a sweeping of the Spirit's fire?" J. Goforth—*When the Spirit's Fire Swept Korea*, p. 69.

19. What were some of the lasting effects of Goforth's revival in the churches of China? Marshall Broom Hall—*The Jubilee Story of the China Inland Mission*, pp. 272-273.

20. How was Goforth's faith in Zechariah 4:2 evidenced in the work with the young people of Shantung? J. Goforth—*By My Spirit*, pp. 146-164.

21. Mrs. Goforth was a woman of prayer. Note her scriptural basis for an "abiding" prayer life. R. Goforth—*How I Know God Answers Prayer*, pp. 129-130.

22. In what way do the examples of answered prayer listed in chapter eight of the above text prove the truth that "All things are possible with God?" R. Goforth—*How I know God Answers Prayer*, pp. 105-123.

23. Discuss the trials and joys of a missionary wife and mother. R. Goforth—*Chinese Diamonds for the King of Kings*, pp. 45-47.

24. Describe some of the chief phases of heathenism. R. Goforth—*Chinese Diamonds for the King of Kings*, pp. 71-77.

25. Did Goforth's blindness greatly hinder his work? Why? R. Goforth—*Goforth of China*, pp. 322-323.

26. What was Goforth's activity on returning home as a "retired missionary?" R. Goforth—*Goforth of China*, pp. 337-339.

CPSIA information can be obtained
at www.ICGtesting.com
Printed in the USA
FFHW010631050819
54051711-59771FF